A Gringo in Milparada

Life in a Village of Squatters

Richard Galbraith

A Gringo in Milparada: Life in a Village of Squatters

Copyright ©2010 by Richard Galbraith

ISBN: 1453643567

EAN-13: 9781453643563

Printed in the U.S.A.

First Printing

Introduction

What happens when a small group of idealistic college students are confronted by the realities of life in a village of subsistence farmers? I went looking for an adventure and a chance to understand a different culture. I could not have foreseen all of the frustrations or joyful moments that ensued. We struggled to make a positive impact on the villagers. We had some successes, and some disappointments.

The biggest surprise was how deeply the people let me enter into their lives. We were accepted as friends, given lots of help and appreciation for our efforts. With a few of the families, our relationship grew into what can only be described as mutual love.

I did not discover any answer for the problems of poverty in Central America. I did come away with a vastly changed perspective of the world. This is the unvarnished account of my adventure and discoveries.

Adventure in Honduras

Sunday, June 20

I have just turned nineteen and finished my freshman year at Cornell University. I've never kept a diary before, but I'm setting out on the adventure of a lifetime and I want to remember it all as it unfolds.

I am part of a group of eight students who will be spending the summer living in a village of subsistence farmers in rural Honduras. We will be attempting Peace Corps style community development projects while promoting good will and understanding. At the end of the project, I plan to spend the last two weeks of summer to bus/hitchhike up the Pan American highway with a side trip to Vera Cruz, then to Mexico City and on up to El Paso, Texas.

It was the altruistic spirit of the Peace Corps that initially attracted me to the project. We will be following their model of community development, helping the locals learn to help themselves. Our prime sponsor is the Cornell United Religious Works, so the planning and administration is done by some of the chaplains. They promote the program as increasing international understanding and good will.

I have some selfish motives as well. I am deeply curious about life in a different culture, especially in understanding how the poor live. Plus, I want to prove to myself that I can manage to get by in foreign country, without modern conveniences and with being forced to communicate in Spanish. (I hope that my three years of high school Spanish plus one year in college is sufficient.) My Dad still talks about his experiences in Panama in 1940 and 1941. I want an adventure of my own.

Still it was a tough choice, mainly because I'll be spending money this summer instead of making it. Dad is helping with the direct cost, but I had been planning on netting at least five hundred dollars from a summer job. Without that pad, I'm going to have to squeeze through next year on a worse than no-frills budget. I'll get by somehow.

We have been preparing for the trip for an entire semester. The seminars and reading amounted to a full class on Latin American history and anthropology. The practical training was minimal. We had one weekend at a camp where we tried out our meal preparation skills by chopping the head off of a chicken with a hatchet, plucking it then cooking chicken with rice and beans over kerosene burners. Most of the rest of that weekend focused on health dangers and precautions for avoiding problems in the tropics. I'm not sure of how realistic the training has been. Time will tell.

Tuesday, June 22

The bus arrived in Miami about 2:00 pm yesterday. I checked into a cheap downtown hotel (the Lindsay Hopkins) which had been recommended by one of the students who made the trip last year. For $3.50 a night, I got a small comfortable single room with the bathroom down the hall. The hotel has a small Japanese Garden, but not much else in the way of amenities.

I spent the rest of the afternoon walking around the area. The weather is uncomfortably hot and muggy. The nearest residential area is a slum crammed with tiny wooden shacks. Nearly all of the people I encountered were Cubans. After a hot dog and Coke from a street vendor I came across a lit baseball field and sat in the bleachers to watch the game. I tried to eavesdrop on the Spanish conversations going on around me. I was only able to pick out a few words. This does not bode well for getting along in Honduras.

The plane leaves early tomorrow morning. I had a day to kill with no commitments. The Gray Line offerings struck me as not very exciting and over my budget, so I tried to do a little sightseeing on my own.

I took a local bus over to Miami Beach, to see the glamorous part of the area. That was a disappointment. The long strip of beach front hotels was rather unattractive and monotonous. The row of white buildings with light blue trim reminded me of hospitals. They form a barricade between the street and the beach, so if there is a nice part to this resort, it is blocked from public view. When I finally reached a public beach, it was shabby, with very little sand. The surf was minimal compared to California and the water was dirty. I needed to find something better if I was going to get my mind off of worrying about tomorrow.

After lunch, I browsed the Bass Art Museum. It was good for a couple of hours of browsing. I particularly like a pair of huge, fantastically life-like tapestries: "Before the Hunt" and "After the Hunt."

I'm back in my hotel room after a boring dinner and a refreshing shower. Now it is "early to bed, early to rise." I hope I don't have any problems getting to the plane on time.

Wednesday, June 23

This is the real first day of our adventure. I got up at 4:30am and took a cab to the airport, arriving at 5:30am to meet up with the rest of the team. It was a relief to see they were all here.

Our team leader is Juan; he is a native of Costa Rica who just got his degree in Agricultural Economics. He'll be returning to Cornell for graduate work next year. Our next-senior member is Melissa, who has just become a Registered Nurse. She will be the first certified medical person to visit the village. Mary has just completed her first year of nursing school and will be assisting in the health and nutrition program. Ed is a Spanish major, so he is the designated lead for organizing our literacy classes. Doug is an English major who spent last summer working on a Forest Service crew. Sue has finished her junior year, and is designated to coordinate English classes. Katrina is a History major, in charge of the recreation program for the children. If we had met under different circumstances, I would be trying to date Katrina. However, since we need to be working together as a unified team, dating within the group is taboo. Probably just as well for me, because I would probably lose out to Doug or Ed. Anyways, since I play the guitar (somewhat), I'm the designated coordinator for entertainment, whatever that turns out to be, and I am also the treasurer for the team funds, probably because nobody else would take the job. We have a budget of $720 dollars, about eleven dollars per week per person to cover our basic living expenses: food, local transportation, supplies and equipment. We will have a very basic life-style.

It was a cheerful reunion, until Doug got to the check-in counter. The information on his visa was not an exact match with his passport. Despite our best efforts to vouch for his identity and convince the gate attendant that it was a harmless typo, they wouldn't let Doug board the plane. He would have to see the Honduran Consulate officer in Miami to get it straightened out. It should only take a couple a days, and a few extra dollars. We took off a half-hour late, with seven team members on board. I wonder if we will ever see Doug.

There was not much to see out the window. Due to Castro, the flight path had to detour to avoid flying over Cuba. We made a short stop in Belize. It looked like a thick jungle coming in. The team stayed on board. Most of the passengers got off just long enough to visit the duty-free store. Since Belize is part of the British Commonwealth, Scotch is a bargain - $2.00 a fifth, I was told. The next leg was the most interesting. I could see lots of little islands dotting the Caribbean Sea below us.

Around 11:00am, we landed in Honduras at the San Pedro Sula airport. It is a single runway, with one warehouse, small tower and a hot wooden building for the terminal. A crowd of Rotarians were there to greet us. It took one-half hour to clear the landing check on the tarmac. One heavy-set man with captain's bars on his shirt looked at each passport and typed (by hunt and peck) the passenger's name on his list. Two other soldiers stood around and watched. Once we completed this ritual, we were waved through customs without having to open our luggage. Our Rotarian hosts must have some political clout.

We were driven to the house of Senor William Swanson. (He is a British citizen who owns the tobacco plant. The factory makes several grades of cigarettes for local consumption and exports some of the finer leaves to England.) From the windows on the drive over, San Pedro does not look much different than Miami, except there are uniformed soldiers everywhere. Some are acting as traffic cops (standing on a little platform in the middle of the main intersections to direct the vehicles) and others just loitering around.

The Swanson house is a large single-story home built around an inner courtyard. It has enough bedrooms for all of us, with a bathroom for each two bedrooms. No air-conditioning. The rooms have high ceilings for ventilation. The courtyard has a fountain and lots of plantings. It is a most comfortable accommodation.

A buffet is spread out for our lunch. Nothing exotic was served. We are being treated as distinguished guests. Senor Swanson assures us that we are welcome to stay in his house any time we are in San Pedro over night. After lunch, we enjoy a restful siesta.

This evening we attended the Rotary meeting at a downtown hotel. The meeting was similar to service clubs in the U.S., with a couple of exceptions. Many of the members were gambling before dinner and resumed their games and drinking after the meeting. They freely noted the gambling is illegal, but that law is never enforced. The other difference is that instead of hand shakes, most of the members greeted each other with hardy hugs (*abrazos*). Only about half the members seem to be interested in our projects. Alcalde Borgan is the only one of our sponsors who had been to Milparada. (One other Rotarian admitted to having heard of it.) During the speeches, there was a lot of joking and side talk among the members.

Professional titles seem to be more important here. Introductions and formal addresses included the specific title not just for Doctor, but also for *Engeniero* (Engineer), *Liciendo* (licensed lawyer), *Professor* (any school teacher), *Alcalde* (mayor), and *Don* (generally a landowner, but also a respected elder).

Some of the younger members, Alcalde Antonio Bogran, Engeniero Rafaelito Davila (whose primary employer is Arriba Tropical Radio) and Arnulfo Gutierrez, express a strong sense of social responsibility and see hope for the future realistically. Rafael (the *–ito* added to his first name in the formal introduction translates to Little Rafael or Junior) is a graduate of the University of Miami. According to some of the others, he is the most eligible bachelor in San Pedro and likely to become the next Mayor. He has a reputation for generosity, giving time and money asked (and often when not) even though he is in financial stress (due to his father's health).

He and Arnulfo are the most vocal supporters of the Cornell Project along with Don Lelo Paz, a landowner and dreamer whose grandfather was a President of Honduras. Don Lelo is not a Rotarian, but a fellow guest tonight. His dream is to create *Pueblos Americanos*, bringing together families from all 21 republics in the Western Hemisphere to live together on his land. He seems to know every *campesino* (farmer) in the Quimistan district. He directed almost all the preparations for our stay in Milparada. His father was a Cornell graduate. Don Lelo seems to have been brought up hoping "one day, they come" and improve thing. The gossip is that he was a heavy drinker and has dissipated most of the family's fortune, other than their inherited land. He viewed his life as somewhat wasted until he ran into the Cornell Central America Project, which he claims to be an answer to his prayers. He is definitely atypical – thoroughly organized and insistent. He knows how to get things done, but is very talkative and repetitive. He strikes me as rather narrow minded and slightly senile.

All of the upper class speak English to some degree and have studied abroad (mostly in the U.S.) My first impression of the merchant/upper class in San Pedro is that they socialized as a big happy family. The older members generally seem self-centered, short-sighted. They live for fun and gambling, see no future for Honduras, and keep most of their savings in foreign banks.

As we are driven back, the downtown plaza area is brightly lit and dominated by a Ferris wheel. We have arrived during the Festival of *San Pedro* (Saint Peter). The schools are out for a weeklong celebration. In San Pedro, the carnival features gambling games, a few rides, and a nightly music program, on a temporary stage in front of the plaza. We were told it was kept clean by the fire department "bathing" the operators at 3:00 every morning.

Thursday, June 24

After a good night's sleep and breakfast, we met Nelly Duarte. She is an articulate and independent-minded lady of around thirty. She lives on her father's ranch on the edge of Cofradia, a town part way up the road to Quimistan. She is accompanied by Chito, a long time employee of her family. She is taking Juan to Milparada, to meet some of the town leaders and get an idea of what kind of project should be our top priority. Off they went, with Nelly driving her yellow Ford pickup truck.

The rest of us spent most of the day wandering around, getting oriented to the town and doing some shopping. When we asked our host for his address, so we could tell the taxi drivers where to bring us, he smiled and told us, "Addresses are unimportant here. Most of the people don't know their own. There are no street signs. Cab drivers get confused if you give them street names. They prefer landmarks or prominent building names. The house of Swanson is a prominent building name." He also advised us that there is no tipping in stores or restaurants. "You only give tips in return for special requests or errands. The unemployed boys will be happy to do things in return for a small tip."

San Pedro Sula has a small-town feel to it. Although it is the second largest city in Honduras, the population is only about 70,000. Tegucigalpa is the center of government. San Pedro claims to be the center of commerce. There are no museums or scenic attractions. We pass a number of warehouses and large stores. Many have the same name on them: Canahuate Mercedes, Canahuate Department Store, Canahuate Singer Sewing Machines, Canahuate Jeep. The Canahuates are one of the Arabian families of traders that dominate the export-import business here.

Streets are mostly narrow one-way meandering routes with no signs. There are a three stop lights near the central plaza. These are viewed more as status symbols than as traffic control devices. It is a matter of pride that San Pedro has one more traffic light than the capital city of Tegucigalpa. The plaza is flanked by the cathedral, municipal building and the main market place. Downtown is reasonably clean; there are some beggars, but not too many (and they are reasonably clean also).

The upper classes shop in modern stores and the supermarket on side streets. The market place is for the common folks. People around the market tense up when a well-dressed person walks by. Well-dressed refers to nice sports clothes; I don't see any suits or ties. The soldiers around the plaza are pompous loafers, cradling their submachine guns in their arms as they swagger around or smoke.

I am surprised not to see any bananas in the market. It turns out that they are all picked when green so that they ripen on the ships. Even though it is the largest crop in Honduras, the closest things available for local consumption are *plantanos* (plantains – a larger, starchier cousin that must be cooked before eating). The retail markup is high. The farmers sell their beans to dealers for eight cents a pound and the grocery stores re-sell them for twenty-five. In the open market, these prices come down somewhat with bargaining. Shoes are available for ten *Lempira* ($ 5) a pair. Locally-made shirt sell for the equivalent of two to three dollars, compared to ten dollars for shirts imported from the U.S. Levis are a luxury items, costing more here than in the U.S., with the import taxes and freight doubling the cost. Local cigarettes are available for as low as a nickel a pack – the cheapest brand is *Buffalos*, with an emblem matching the buffalo on the old American nickels.

Most stores close between 11:30am and noon, then reopen in mid-afternoon. Since the water is impure, we drink coffee, Coca Cola or beer. Coca Cola signs are everywhere.

The most striking thing about San Pedro is the large amount of building going on. Times are good and San Pedro is growing. This afternoon, we met Mr. Kane, an American architect working on the Union Housing Project. He showed us around his project, financed by the AFL-CIO based on instigation of two local labor union leaders. They are creating a development of 1,200 houses with water, electricity and sewage utilities on land obtained from the government. The houses are concrete block with a main room, bedroom, kitchen and small bathroom. The houses cost $2,200 to $3,200 to be paid for at $30 to $50 a month. The payments are comparable to the rent on the wooden houses (without plumbing or electricity) United Fruit supplies for its field workers. The pilot project had 120 completed houses, each with a couple of banana trees planted in the small yard. They all look neatly kept, but then, they are new.

The rainy season has just started. The climate is very hot and sticky from late morning through the afternoon. It is comfortable in the evenings. It rains from about 3:00-5:00 intermittently every afternoon, with a few heavy downpours. I haven't heard any thunder, and apparently winds are only a problem if a hurricane comes through.

At dinner, Juan reported to us on his visit. Nelly Duarte has been helping Cornell teams for several years. She stored all of the equipment left by last year's Quimistan team on her father's ranch. They stopped by the ranch and loaded the twelve folding cots and burlap bags full of kitchen equipment and hand tools into the back of her pick up. All of that stuff is now locked in the school building. When they got to Milparada, she introduced Juan to Pedro Hernandez and Antonio Machado. Pedro is only about twenty-five, but is still apparently one of the most respected people in the area. Pedro was a leader in working with the Quimistan team last year to get the Milparada school building completed. He is eager to cooperate with this year's team. Antonio struck him as an intelligent, clear thinker in spite of having very little education. Antonio expressed a true preoccupation with the need to improve the community. Both men recognize that we have made a sacrifice in coming to Honduras, not out of pride, but because we believe that the people should have a better life. Antonio emphasized the last point and said that our manner of living could make changes in Milparada. Pedro emphasized the importance of the school to the community. Both agreed that the most important thing was to improve things for the children.

We have quite a reputation to live up to. It is going to be a challenge.

Friday, June 25

Today was filled with meetings and planning. Rafael is our host and guide for the day. His VW bus is our transportation.

8:30 am: We start at the American Consulate. Consul Tom Killoran is a good man. He has been here for years, knows the country well and is well-liked (according to Rafael). Still his Spanish seems a little weak. Most of what he tells us just confirms the things we had read about Honduras before we came down.

10:00: Visit Bicultural Center. Its principle function is teaching English classes. The classes are popular because speaking English is seen as a passport to the better paying jobs.

11:00: Visit *Mission Evangelica*. The Evangelical mission has been active here since 1921. It is headed by John Will. He strikes me as very intelligent and dedicated, rather shy. Although they were founded to spread the Gospel, most of their energy is spent on education in the broader sense. Their missions provide the best schools (grades 1-6) in the country. Their mission in Pinalejo is within walking distance of Milparada. The missionaries also distribute literacy material based largely on phonetic association between the letters and pictures of common objects. He will be happy to supply us with some sets of these *Alfalit* pamphlets. We will use for them for adult education tutoring. Their missions also provide medical services. He stated flatly that there is almost no cooperation or coordination between the different religious groups that have missions here. Even though the Catholic Church does not have enough priests to go around, they tend to see the missions as competitors, rather than as fellow Christians.

2:00 pm: Rafael gives us a tour of the art exhibit in the *Palacio Municipal*. Some of the paintings are good work, but they offer very little local flavor.

2:30 pm: Meeting at the CARE offices. The local director, John Moran is modest, efficient, and very helpful. CARE will supply us with materials for building school desk. Of more interest is the program for distributing commodities for the school lunch centers. The food is free to any school with a facility and organization that maintains adequate controls over the hygienic preparation and accounting for the food. This sounds like a perfect fit for our efforts in Milparada.

3:30 pm: Formal meeting with mayor - Alcalde Borgan. He is a very partisan politician. He explained, "All liberal parties are run by communists ranging from pale pink to bright red." Nevertheless, he is intelligent and hard working and sees the necessity of a social revolution to improve the lot of the *campesinos*. Improving the rural conditions will keep the communists from attracting support.

4:30 pm: Visit the *Exposicion de Industrias Pequenas*. This is an exhibit that is intended to promote opportunities for small business, as part of the Festival of San Pedro. There were lots of people looking, but very little to see.

Dinner was followed by a long talk with Rafael and Guillermo Swanson. (Senor Swanson goes by the Spanish version of William most of the time.) They have had trouble getting real support from the Rotary Club. The communications of results have been vague. They need more concrete reports and evidence of the project's accomplishment.

The establishment of a *Comedor Infantil* (children's eating center) in Milparada has increased all of our enthusiasm. Rafael offered to make sketches for the construction of the *comedor* and latrines and showers for the school and our houses. He also promised to obtain for us 40 bags of cement, asbestos roofing and wood for the construction.

After Rafael left, Senor cautioned us that people here commonly offer more that they can deliver. Specifically, Rafael had recently offered the use of his car to two different groups planning to go to different towns at the same time.

I must say that the coffee here, served with sugar and no cream, is far superior to the stuff we get in New York. Also, the local beer, *Cervesa Nacional* tastes better (and stronger) than its U.S. counterparts.

P.S. Good news: We got a telegram from Doug. His visa is straightened out and he will be arriving on tomorrow's plane.

Saturday, June 26

I had a leisurely morning. I took a cab from Swansons' house to the airport at 9:30 am, only to have a long wait. Doug's plane was an hour late getting in. The ride to the airport cost *Lempira* 1.50 (75 cents), but the return trip cost twice that. It wasn't because of the extra passenger. The extra *L*1.50 is a fee the driver has to pay the airport when he picks someone up. I asked him if we had walked the two blocks to the airport gate, would he get the *L*1.50 rate. He said no. From outside the airport the fee is only *L*0.50, but the driver would feel cheated and might not pick us up there.

We spent the afternoon on the porch of the Hotel Columbia listening to Don Lelo. He says that the Hotel Bolivar is good, but it is priced for tourists. He names a couple of other hotels we might be interested in because they provide a girl with each room. He tells us that they are safe and legal. The licensed girls get a medical exam and penicillin shot every week. Those facilities are outside of both my budget and my interests.

Since Doug was freshly arrived, he started over with a full description of his dreams and hopes for the future. He is not happy with the new government, even though he is of the same party. He said that President General Lopez really has the support of only five to ten percent of the population. He is aloof and dictatorial. He runs the army, and that is all he needs for now.

Don Lelo was speaking entirely in Spanish. Listening is good practice, but still a strain. I am still thinking in English and translating my thoughts. In any case, I was getting bored with all this hanging around and doing little except talk. I am impatient to get to Milparada and the main experience.

Rafael Davila drove us to a small private club for evening drinks. We were relaxing over beers (except for Melissa, who doesn't drink) on the veranda, when Sue asked, "What's that?" That brought our attention to a rat the size of a house cat scurrying across a rafter. Rafael just shrugged. Nobody except us gringos paid it any attention.

I have seen no sign of any ostentatious wealth in San Pedro. Except for the presence of servants (in lieu of labor-saving devices), the lifestyle of the upper class seems equivalent to U.S. professionals. Maybe they enjoy their luxuries in private or when they travel abroad.

Sunday, June 27

We left San Pedro Sula at 9:30 this morning in a *"busito"* (VW bus). Rafael drove and Nelly Duarte followed in her pickup truck loaded with the wood for twenty-five CARE desks and most of our luggage.

For the first half-hour, the road is a well-graded two lane road, except where it crosses the Chamelecon River. There the cars and trucks share a single lane railroad bridge. The land around us is lush and green. Once across the river, the road winds along the hillside. We stopped at *"Boca de Caballo"*, a dangerous turn in the road where a *"busito"* with four passengers had recently left the road to land some 60 feet down into the gorge. Looking out the window, I caught my first sight of slash and burn farming: a patch of scorched ground with black tree trunks on a steep hillside. It stood in stark contrast to the surrounding jungle. I wonder how you plough such a steep field.

We stopped at Quimistan. This was the site of last year's Cornell team. It is a drab and dusty town with about 1,000 residents. Still, it is an official municipality with jurisdiction over the surrounding district. It has a post office, which gets mail on Tuesdays and Thursdays, a general store, and a restaurant that also has a couple of rooms to rent. The two main employers are the kiln, which makes roofing tiles and a *tobacalero* (a facility where tobacco leaves are sorted). Most of the buildings in the center of town have concrete floors and have been painted. The town has electricity in the early evening, provided by a diesel generator.

We picked up Don Castillo, the mayor, to join us for our formal introduction to the people of Milparada. Leaving the main road, we follow a single lane track. This is the road less traveled; there is grass growing between the tire ruts. The track is bordered by a row of small trees on each side, with strands of barbed wire making a fence. Don Lelo explained that they were put there as fence posts and took root with all the tropical warmth and rain.

We crossed a stream where some women with small children were doing laundry on the rocks. Don Lelo encourages us with the information that after a heavy rain, the river gets deeper and you can't cross it for several days. As we come up the opposite bank, we enter the village.

The school building dominates the entrance to the village. It is a simple rectangle, but with ten-foot-tall walls of large grey bricks, it is much larger than the surrounding houses. A weed strewn triangular patch of ground in front of the school serves as the town's plaza.

We are introduced to Don Pedro Hernandez and several other members of the community. All the villagers seem to know Don Lelo. Other than the two school teachers and the "*Alcalde Auxiliar*" (auxiliary mayor), a post that is passed around among the young men in the town, there are no representatives of the government in the village. We "seal the deal" on constructing a *comedor* as an extension of the school. It will be a simple structure that can be built in a few weeks. Don Lelo and Don Pedro took us on a walking tour of the village. We are followed by a pack of curious children, mostly watching us from a safe distance. Don Lelo did most of the talking. He estimates the population as about three hundred. Everyone here is a squatter, growing corn and beans to feed his family; none of them legally own their homes or farms. The name Milparada is a shortened form of *milpa arada*, or ploughed cornfield. The typical field is about three *manzanas* (five acres) for a family of six. The town boasts two small stores, both are which occupy part of the main room of a house. The town has no church or patron saint and had never been visited by a priest, doctor, or nurse. Chickens and small dogs wander around the town. The water system is a one-inch pipe carrying water down from the mountains to Quimistan. There are two public faucets, one at the end of the plaza and the other near the far end of town. The residents are allowed to tap into the line and run a water pipe to their own house. The few who can afford to buy the pipe have their own private faucet. There are no outhouses; the people just go in the bushes. There is one exception. They have dug a pit and built a one-hole bench over it in back of one of the two houses we will occupy. The village is certainly rustic. Our stay will be like a long camping trip. That is fine by me, but some of the girls seemed worried about how primitive our conditions are.

The team will live in two small mud houses. At present, both have dirt floors. The project's standard for housing a team requires an improved floor (for sanitary reasons, primarily to keep us from getting infected by hook worms) and a water supply in addition to a latrine. The improvements were also promised to the home owners in lieu of rent. I am concerned about displacing two families, but am told that one of the owners also has another home and the other is staying with relatives. We will have to make the improvements before moving in. Since school is out for the Festival of San Pedro, we will live in the school this week.

The larger house will serve as our headquarters. It has a single room with an adobe wood-burning stove at one end. By hanging a curtain from a rafter, we will be able to separate the girls' sleeping quarters holding cots from the kitchen/dining room. The other house has two rooms: one just large enough to hold five cots for the boys' sleeping quarters. We will use the other room (kitchen) for storage and desk building/painting.

We had lunch, or rather were honored with chicken and tortillas at Pedro Hernandez's house. This is the first time either Melissa or Trinchi has tried a tortilla. (Don Lelo gave Katrina the nickname Trinchi, and it stuck.) The local tortillas are thicker than the ones I am used to in Mexican restaurants, probably because they are entirely formed by hand. He has the nicest looking house in town. It is L-shaped, and has a brick floored, somewhat shady patio with some flowering bougainvilleas. We ate at a picnic table set up on the patio. We were served by two women of about the same age and joined by a quiet teenage boy; I'm not sure how they are related to Pedro.

In the afternoon, we inventoried our supplies (most of which had been left by the prior year's team in storage at Nelly's ranch). We set up a Lister bag (with a capacity of thirty gallons), fired up the kerosene stoves and started boiling a supply of water.

I went with Nelly to get lime from the nearby village of Pinalejo. We drove into Quimistan, dropped off *Alcalde* Castillo, and took a somewhat better road to the northwest. There is a direct path between Pinalejo and Milparada, but it is supposedly too rutted for normal cars. Pinalejo is a small village but is very pretty in comparison to Milparada. One side of the road is dominated by the white mission and mission school. The church building has never been completed, but no construction is going on. Maybe the incomplete state of the church is a symbolic statement, like the unfinished bell tower at the San Xavier Mission in Tucson. In any case, the church is too large for the size of the town. A slightly sloped clearing across the road serves as a landing strip for occasional small planes. Chito and I loaded two oil drums full of powdered lime into the back of the truck. The lime will be the base for whitewashing our houses, plus a little in the latrine to prevent it from being a breeding ground for bugs.

The rain was coming down hard when we got back to Quimistan, so we waited it out at Don Castillo's house, before returning to Milparada. A number of villagers were hanging out near the school watching the activities of the team as we set up camp in the school. About 4:30pm, Nelly and Rafael left. Rafael promised to get us a couple of bicycles so we could get around faster. Given the uneven terrain, I'm not sure bikes will be practical.

We had supper at Don Pedro Hernandez's house. Don Pedro Hernandez seems to be very sincere and cooperative. At supper time, he gave a beautiful grace, thanking God for our food and the presence of the Cornell Team. During dinner he told us that all of the villages are very conscious of their poverty and consider it their natural state in the world. He says there is a famous phrase "poverty breeds poverty." Thus tradition and acceptance of fate are principal reasons for their present state. Juan asked if he thought the people could change their state. Pedro paused in thought before replying. "I believe that, but the important thing to do in this town is to improve the school. The school must be attractive. If the school is pretty the town also is." He is very enthusiastic about the planned construction of the school dining room and also understands that without a responsible committee or people who take charge themselves to continue our work, everything will be lost.

Afterwards, we had an audience of about twenty-five, so Melissa and I played the Honduran National Anthem (Melissa on flute). Then I continued with a few folk songs in English and Spanish. I guess that is going to have to pass for our "entertainment" program.

I can't tell what everyone on the team is feeling. We are keeping a positive outward demeanor, but it is obvious that most of us were impressed by the level of poverty of the people in Milparada. There is a lot of work to be done and we plan to start tomorrow.

Don Lelo is staying over in the school with us, sleeping on one of the spare cots. He assured us that he never snored, but five minutes later he was sawing logs. His noise was soon drowned out by Juan. I'm having troubled drifting off.

Monday, June 28

Tomorrow has now arrived and our first day in Milparada is past. Much to my surprise the night was quite cold. We woke up extra early. Ed had set the alarm clock wrong so it went off at 4:30 (an hour early). We stumbled around in the dark getting ready for the day. Several other team members commented on the cold, so it wasn't just me.

Because we are staying in the school until "our houses" are ready and because we are still completely discombobulated and because the Hernandez's are so cordial, we had all three meals there.

In the morning we boys worked on laying pipe from the water tap in the plaza to our houses. We had a pickaxe and a pair of shovels to dig a trench about a foot deep. The hard work had us consuming quarts of water, acquiring blisters and making friends with the village plumber and a couple of helpers. Don Lelo supervised and pitched with the heavy work. The girls spent most of the day sorting, washing, boiling and getting the plates ready for use. Their work was frequently interrupted by mothers who came "to call" and – needless to say – many children who merely came to look and try to figure out what the crazy gringos were doing.

The afternoon came and went in much the same manner. We got the water to the back of what will be the girls' house with a spigot by the kitchen window. We also assembled a wooden latrine over a six foot hole in the ground. The houses are still unfinished wood floors, so we will have to cement them to prevent fungus and parasite problems. The girls got the backyards raked up and had a chance to try their (limited) Spanish by reading with the children. Our houses don't have front yards – the doors open right on to the "plaza"/soccer field. For dinner, once more we sponged off the Hernadezs'. They are tremendously gracious – for what they give us is all they have and are able to give. Pedro is our primary host, but we are getting to appreciate the entire family.

Pedro Hernandez is 25 and completed six years of schooling, walking daily to Pinalejo for the last three. He knows geography well, including the location of our home States in the U.S. and is anxious to learn English. He has one son and a trial wife. They hope for a church wedding someday. Consciously the town leader, he wants to impress us with his abilities. He "knows" how to do anything we asked about. But then again, he is optimistic about everything. He told us that he plans on being rich next year. They are the only Protestant family in town and go to the mission church in Pinalejo a couple of times a month. (Quimistan has a Catholic church, but a priest only gets there once every two months. So occasionally some of the other townspeople go with him.) Politically he is a Nationalist, telling us: "The liberals are communists" and referring to Castro as "the assassin in Cuba."

His father, Juan Z. Hernandez shares the house with him. At fifty years old, he is a senior citizen – dignified and quiet, but still works the fields with Pedro. He doesn't have much to do with us. In addition to their large cornfield, *Don* Juan owns twenty *manzanas* (about thirty-five acres) of coffee in the mountains. That is enough land to earn the respectful title of *Don*, even though they don't have proper titles to their land. He also owns fifteen milk cows which pasture on the ranch of Don Medardo Florentino (a well off resident of Pinalejo). Don Medardo has recently gotten tractors to construct a good road to his ranch, which also makes it easier for Juan and Pedro to ship out their coffee harvest.

The teenager, also named Juan Hernandez, turns out to be Pedro's brother. He is fourteen, but is tall for his age (at least by local standards). Around us, he is quiet and attentive, trying to absorb all that is going on, but seems rather passive. I haven't seen him playing soccer with the other teens. He says he is working hard at learning English and claims he was a good friend of Tutico (Stuart, who was on the Cornell team in Quimistan last year).

Pedro's sister seems to do most of the housework, but his wife, and an older woman who is probably his mother (she was not introduced to us) and several other women wander in and out plying us with tortillas and coffee – the main staples of their diets. Evening passed much as before. I played the guitar and we all made sad attempts to sing. If we didn't entertain them, we couldn't have helped but amuse them. We went back to our cots at 9:15.

We are definitely a curiosity. Based on one day of experience, we are objects of interest, excitement and bewilderment. The children are the least shy and because they are on vacation, spend every minute staring with open eyes and listening with open ears to our strange doings – such as building a place to go to the bathroom, boiling plates, drinking green water (Kool-Aid), taking pills and speaking absolute gibberish. The men come over to talk to us in the evening. The woman's place is subservient and in the house. During the day, many of the women offered to teach our girls how to make tortillas.

Milparada is a quiet village; as the teacher says "Milparada has nothing except the school" – no church, no stores, no library, no electricity. Yet it is a village which has people who want to learn and want to help us to learn. Whatever we accomplish here, I hope we can engender some pride in their community. The town is not beautiful in itself, but beautiful in its surroundings and in its people.

Tuesday, June 29

Today started at 5:30 am – daybreak. We had breakfast at 6:00 at Pedro's home. This was our last meal at Pedro's. It turns out that the table on the patio had been made for us by some of the Rotarians in San Pedro. We carried the table and our two chairs back to the school.

Today was a day of physical labor. The other guys finished extending the water line to make a shower in the back yard with a seven-foot vertical pipe. There is no enclosure, so showering will be done in swimsuits. I joined three of the local men in the oxcart, going down the river to gather sand. Antonio provided his oxcart. The two wheels are wooden disks (two semi-circles bolted together) with a crooked axle, so one wheel rubbed the side. Traveling by oxcart is much slower than walking.

The bed of the oxcart is over three feet off the ground and we were standing down in the stream bed, so we had to lift our shovels to shoulder height to load the sand. It was hard for me to keep up with the helpers. The one with the long-handled shovel had an obvious advantage of leverage in tossing sand over the two of us with short-handled spades. The slow trips back up to the village were a welcome respite from the shoveling.

The girls continued to clean the supplies (which had been stored in a shed in Quimistan since last summer). Their water hauling drew a following of children. Some of the town's girls offered to carry the loads when the team members were looking weary and pausing to rest. Making lunch had turned out to be a real project – boiling enough water for washing vegetables, drinking, and rinsing the dishes took a long time over our four small kerosene burners. The sand duty made me late for lunch. Still, everyone was in good spirits and the plate full of rice with tomatoes, onions, and cheese with bread and Kool-Aid on the side tasted good, even cold.

The plumber turned off the water on the main line and made the final connection. There were no leaks when he turned it back on. Our first construction task is complete.

We spent the afternoon leveling the dirt floor and laying a base layer of sand in the girls' house. Antonio made a tamper with green wood for us to compact the sand. It is staggeringly heavy.

Soon it was 4:00pm – time for the official town meeting with us at the school. By the time enough of the men had returned from the fields to begin it was 5:15, but in the meantime we had a good opportunity to get acquainted with people we hadn't met yet. With a total audience of about eighty adults, Don Pedro welcomed us sincerely and beautifully. The school children sang the Honduran national anthem then we sang the *Star Spangled*

Banner in return. Ed gave a short talk explaining our purpose here. Don Lelo spoke words of praise for the group, but made it clear that we are here to be equal with the people.

After the meeting, dinner was prepared. We ate by lantern light. After dinner, the girls held flashlights for us while we finished preparing their floor for cement. It was completely dark by the time we finished. Then we (boys first) changed into our swim suits and flip-flops and tried out our shower. It provided little more than a drizzle, but after three days in the tropics, the shower was a major relief.

We are ending the evening gathered around our table. The beans for tomorrow's meals are soaking in a big pot. We are planning tomorrow's work, and concurrently practicing our Spanish. We have decided to minimize our use of English even among ourselves. I just finished writing my first letter home. With the tropical humidity, the stamps and envelope flaps are always sticky, so they hardly need licking.

Today I have seen the team really working together as a team – cooperation, team spirit, a real desire to communicate with the people. This promises to be a very splendid summer.

Wednesday, June 30

The alarm clock was set for 5:30, but it was nearly 6:30 before everyone was up and moving. My clothes felt clammy, even fresh from the suit case; nothing ever gets really dry here.

The previous day's work must have been too much for some of the weaker members of the team! This was the first day that we had breakfast in the school – scrambled eggs, toast and coffee, prepared by the girls.

Immediately after breakfast, the boys resumed work putting in cement floors. Ten sacks of cement were transferred from Pedro's house to the site of construction with the help of a wheelbarrow borrowed from one of our neighbors. Now all the materials and tools were ready, but the actual work was delayed while we debated the best sand-cement ratio, thickness of the floor and our mixing/pouring methods. We wanted an adequate floor with the least amount of materials (particularly "costly" cement) and labor. We also discovered that we did not have the proper tools. Specifically, our equipment did not include a single trowel. Antonio came to the rescue, making a wooden trowel. We ended up mixing the cement in our galvanized steel laundry tub and spreading it with a shovel and Antonio's invention.

Meanwhile, the girls had collected all the dirty clothes and took them down to the river to wash them with the local ladies. This method of cleaning clothes seems to be as effective as the machine-age method – the clothes came out clean, anyway. According to the girls, food preparation is almost a day's job in itself. The quality of our food may not attest to this fact, even though the meals have been excellent considering working conditions, etc. Lunch included a very tasty soup and rice. The boys will begin taking turns cooking as soon as we move into the houses, hopefully Friday night, or Saturday morning at the latest.

Pedro came in after lunch was over and talked with those of us who chose to pass up a siesta. About 2 pm the boys returned to the house to continue laying cement while the girls finished the cleaning chores. The cement work progressed slowly but surely – a little slower than we had anticipated. Pedro offered his services for the entire afternoon and some of the other members of the community stopped by when they got in from their fields to render help if it was needed. With the extra hands (including the girls in our team – to the surprise of the locals), we got a good start on preparing the floor of the boys' house as well. By 5:15, we had completed the floor of the girls' house and decided that this would be a good place and time to stop for the day. Although I may be prejudiced, it is my opinion that the floor looked great, especially considering the circumstances and the limited tools we had. In any case, it is the best (and first) cement work that I had ever done. We are all proud of this material achievement, as it is a contribution which will outlive our short stay here. It makes the sore backs seem worthwhile.

Dinner tonight was exceptional – the best meal we have had since our arrival. The girls must be getting the hang of the gas stove, Honduran food, etc. The children continue to stare curiously through the windows during mealtimes, even though I can't recognize anything strange or extraordinary about our eating habits, table manners or types of food. (Perhaps it is purely the quantity of food we eat – while we are using simple, locally available ingredients, the portions are generous.) Perhaps this phenomenon will last all summer – Members of last year's team had commented on the lack of privacy during our training.

We seem to have a little better direction and organization in our work now, and cooperation with respect to the people living here is at a maximum level. Generally, the work is progressing well and everyone seems fairly optimistic.

Thursday, July 1

The alarm went off at 5:30 again, but many of us were so tired that we didn't hear it, or at least didn't react to it. Consequently we weren't finished with breakfast until about 7:00 am. Breakfast was – as were all three meals today – a rather "come as you are" meal – that is we ate what we had on hand and didn't try any great, new fangled ideas. The girls are getting rather tire of cooking and washing dishes and will be glad when we can move into our houses and can cook inside without an audience of "gringo watchers". This evening when Sue and Mary were cooking with some children watching (the rest of the team were talking with Don Pedro and his sisters), poor Sue dropped the hot lids several times and once the dish towel she was using as a potholder caught fire. Everyone (except Sue) got a big charge out of ensuing commotion.

This morning went very slowly for the girls while the boys were busy. We poured the concrete floor in the boys' bedroom. Tomorrow, we will be able to whitewash the walls and have the girls' house ready to move in. Trinchi and Ed walked into Quimistan this morning and got needed groceries and MAIL. Don Lelo went with them and stayed through the afternoon visiting friends. It is a forty-five minute walk one way at a good even clip. The rest of the girls decided to put some school desks together, but found out that we needed a drill in order to make holes for the screws, so that plan was abandoned.

Melissa and Mary held an informal clinic. They cleaned and redressed the foot of Julia, a girl who had cut it on a rock, replacing a filthy rag with a nice white bandage. Julia left with a proud smile on her face. Next a mother with a seven month old baby came in and wanted them to do something for the baby who she said had asthma. The baby had phlegm in his chest and what looked like the beginning of a rash on his stomach. Melissa thinks this baby is coming down with chicken pox, of which there is currently an epidemic in the area. Also, the mother has grippe, so the baby could have that too. There was nothing we could do for the baby except to tell the mother to give him a lot of liquids and if he develops a fever to put a cold rag on the baby's head. We also told her to put the baby on his stomach when sleeping. As Mary took the baby and was trying to show her the positioning, the baby peed all over her dress and the bench! We told her to take the baby to see the Doctor in Quimistan, but even though she nodded her head, her expression indicated that she wouldn't. (Seeing a doctor, even in the clinic costs money.) Later another mother came with a sick baby with similar symptoms, and was given the same advice. Several of the patients need treatment beyond what our nurses can supply, but they felt they had to do the best they could and provide some assistance to avoid losing their trust.

After lunch, the boys took a short siesta while the girls cleaned up the dishes. Then the boys went back to work. We poured the floor of the kitchen/storeroom in the boys' house. We had two helpers (Antonio and a friend) all day, so the work went easier than yesterday. Antonio is a master at smoothing the concrete with his wooden trowel.

The girls went hunting a place to bathe. Doug had said the he had taken a bath in water up to his waist, but didn't give directions. I haven't seen anyplace where the river is more than a few inches deep. The girls walked up the river, ducking through the barbed wire fences and along the cow paths, looking for this area. But after going about a half mile without finding the bathing hole, they dammed up some water and created a pool about nine inches deep, which was enough to wash their hair. A line of leaf-cutter ants provided some distraction, with their well organized path from halfway up a tree to their ant hill.

Afterwards the girls were invited by Don Pedro's sister to come to her house to learn to make tortillas. They spent about a half hour trying, but did not master the technique by a long shot. Their first tortillas became part of our dinner and the boys politely said they were pretty good. The local girls all learn about the time they are eleven, and with practice it becomes quick and easy. The corn is first soaked in water with a little lime, then ground with a stone grinder to make a paste/dough ball. Each tortilla is shaped by slapping it between your hands. The tricky part is to get the thickness even. Then it is tossed on to the oil-drum lid that serves as the stove top. In two minutes, it is ready to be flipped over to cook the other side. Senorita Hernandez suggested that if the girls came over each of the next five afternoons, they should master it too. While they were cooking, the dog, cats, chickens and ducks wandered in and out the kitchen at will.

About dinner time, Don Lelo returned with a rabbit that he had shot with his hand gun right out in front of the school. He wanted to know if we wanted to cook it and add it to our dinner. Juan said "Not this time." In response to Lelo's disappointed look, he explained that the girls had already finished cooking. Anotonio was happy to receive the rabbit for his family's dinner.

Today is the first of July. Time is certainly flying as we have been very involved with getting ourselves settled here and with making friends, but we haven't gotten started on our main project. Juan is working with Doug on the plans for the *Comedor Infantil* which we hope to start next week. The floor will need to be eighteen feet wide and about twenty-four feet long, about twice the size of one of our houses.

Another day closes with us sitting around the table, writing and talking. Don Lelo shows great patience in talking to us, speaking slowly and repeating as we struggle with our Spanish.

Friday, July 2

The morning started off earlier than others, if that is possible. Melissa, Don Lelo and I got up at 4 am to walk to Pinalejo and catch the first San Pedro bus. It is actually a locally owned VW bus staffed by a driver and a car man who deals with the fares and passengers. This *busito* left pretty much on schedule, at six with the car man riding in front seat on left side of driver. Don Lelo stayed in Pinalejo to visit with his friends there. The ride was pleasant until we picked up a couple of extra passengers at Chamelecon. They were fishermen with a couple of nets full of (nine to ten inch long) river shrimp they were taking to sell in the San Pedro market. The stench of their catch dominated the last half-hour of the drive.

Our primary purpose was to pick up the *Alfalit* material so we can start our literacy program, and a few hand tools needed to build the desks. We started by trying to find Rafael and then walked to the Evangelical Mission – nobody was there either. Our next stop was a department store, where Melissa picked out enough matching sheets to use as the curtain for the girls' sleeping area. Then I did my shopping at Jorge Larach's hardware store. (He's a Rotarian who gave us a twenty percent discount.) I picked up two trowels for our *comedor* cement work, a hand drill, two drill bits and a good screwdriver for the desks, and bought a machete for myself. The machete is the all-purpose tool for all the *campesinos*, and appears to be more efficient for cutting weeds and chopping fire wood that our team's hoe and hatchet.

Our shopping was followed by another futile round of trying to find Rafael and someone at the Mission. We did successfully meet Arnulfo Gutierrez. He took us to lunch at a pizzeria along with Guillermo Houten, a local student who had gotten permission to skip his two afternoon classes and go to Milparada with us and observe. I had a hearty serving of spaghetti with meat balls and a Coke. Guillermo started talking politics and the need for reform. Arnulfo couldn't remember the name of the Honduran President, "It doesn't make any difference. They change so often and they are all alike." There have been one hundred and forty Presidents, none of whom have completed their official six year term of office.

After lunch, we went to the CARE office to pick up some books and school supplies. We had to wait for more than an hour before anyone came back from the mid-day siesta, only to be told that the materials hadn't arrived yet. "Come back next week. Maybe they will arrive by then." Our third trek to the Mission was successful. We left with three bags of *Alfalit* literacy materials.

After one last attempt to locate Rafael, we went to the market to wait for a bus. We had a long wait. Guillermo and I sipped warm beer in a grubby hole-in-the-wall until the rain stopped. We were accosted by a "hipster" who claimed to be a "Yanqui." He wanted money and a job. I offered neither. The 4:00 bus (an old school bus) didn't arrive and start loading until 5:20. When we went to get on the bus, our bags fell apart (another casualty of the moisture), so wrapped our stuff in the sheets. The bundles made us fit in more with the other passengers. The return trip was further slowed by a stop for gas. The driver got four gallons from an antique gas pump – the kind when the attendant uses a crank to pump the desired amount of gas to a glass section on the top of the pump and then lets gravity drain it into the gas tank. About an hour out, we had a flat tire. Instead of mounting a spare, the driver and car man patched the old tire on the spot and re-inflated it with a bicycle pump. This procedure took an hour.

By the time we were dropped off by the Quismistan clinic, it was pitch black. We hadn't brought a flashlight, so it was an eerie walk back home. Meanwhile, my stomach was bothering me. I had to stop twice to throw up the remains of my spaghetti from lunch.

The others had decided that we must be spending the night in San Pedro, so our 9:00 pm arrival caused quite a commotion. We were treated to a "feast" of stale bread and cheese and got caught up on the activity of the rest of the team before bed.

The rest of the team had gotten up at the usual hour and had oatmeal for breakfast – they reported that I had picked a good meal to miss. Then back to work. The boys almost finished the floors of the second house. The girls whitewashed their house. The white wash greatly improves the looks of the house; however there are problems of durability because the mud walls flake off when you touch them. Pedro helped out in the afternoon. We are becoming increasingly convinced of his exceptional personality. He could not work harder and his complete sincerity and patience with us is amazing and much appreciated. I can't help believing that our work here will go much further in the right direction with the townspeople and even after we leave because of his leadership.

The meals today left quite a bit to be desired – our rations are down to pure starch (which is not far from where they started). For dinner they cooked up some potatoes, rice and bread. Juan helped the dinner conversation by reading from his connoisseur's cook book! It is still a little hard for me to understand the lack of available vegetables when there is so much flourishing greenery around us.

This afternoon, the school from Pinelejo came to look us over. The size of the children surprised the team. All of them are in their early teens and are easily larger than most adults in this village. There must be a large difference in living standards and nutrition unless they are from some hidden cult of giants. The people in Milparada very obviously are aware of the gap between their town and Pinelejo and take it as a blow to their pride. I think the gap in pride is largely based on the prestige of superficial appearances and if we can improve the appearance of Milparada with whitewash and plaster they will take more pride in their homes.

A friend of Don Lelo came with the students. Lelo says he is a millionaire who works and deals in this area. The interesting point (besides his statement that he is the father of twenty-six children) is that he has had no formal education and cannot even add. This must say something as to the character of the Honduran situation, or maybe a sign of how far it has to go.

Tomorrow, the girls will be moving into their house.

Saturday, July 3

Today was rather boring. I loafed all day on instruction from the nurses. Their diagnosis is probable intestinal parasitism (fever of 102, prostration, nausea, vomiting, and diarrhea). My illness is making the team even more health conscious.

Our water for drinking is either boiled or iodized. The iodine leaves a bad taste that Kool-Aid doesn't adequately disguise, so the boiled option is preferable whenever we have the time. A cake of soap was always by the water spigot for hand washing. All team members are conscious of hygiene with thorough hand washing and careful preparation. Cooking with a pressure cooker is a health measure as well as a convenience.

We are careful not to accept gifts of milk or pork (though native cooked chicken is a welcomed treat). Our garbage is emptied into a pit behind the house following each meal and dishes are washed immediately after eating. Dishes were washed in tap water, but rinsed in boiling water. Our nutrition is adequate. Most of our protein comes through beans, eggs and powdered milk. Plus, Melissa doles out our daily vitamin tablets at breakfast. (We also take a weekly chloroquine tablet to prevent malaria.)

The rest of the team finished whitewashing the houses and putting up a couple of shelves. The supply of helpers from the town is still plentiful, but most seem little inclined to work unless provided with an occasional cigarette.

Melissa did some washing in the river.

Trinchi is teaching Pedro English.

A couple of the girls made another abortive attempt to put a desk together. The materials did not come with instructions and much of the wood is at least slightly warped. My sketch of how the parts should fit together didn't solve their problem, but then neither of them have any carpentry experience. Here is what they are supposed to look like:

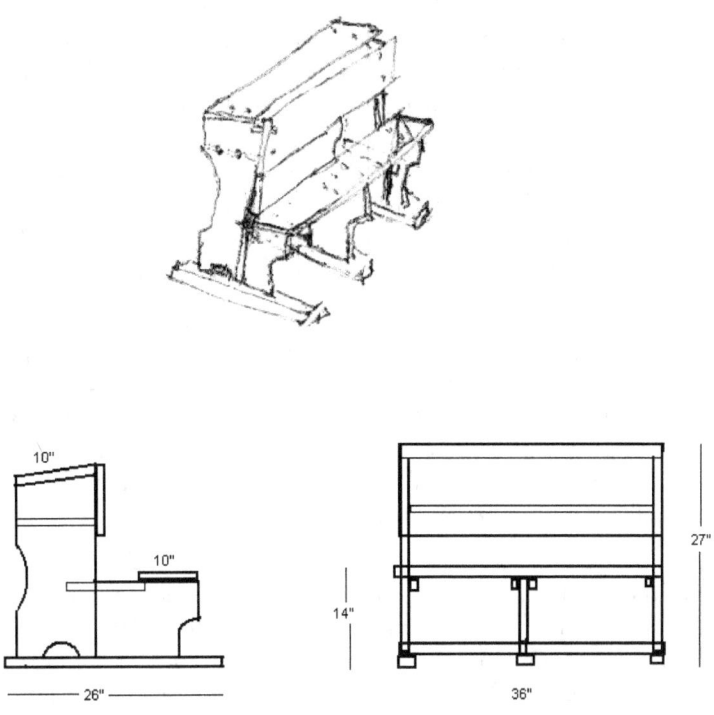

Figure 1. CARE desks

The last time we did some singing, someone asked what the words to "This Land is Your Land" meant. I stumbled after the first line, not sure how to translate "redwood forests" and "Gulf Stream waters." So while lounging on my cot, I worked out a Spanish version customized to reflect our presence in Honduras.

The language barrier hasn't presented any major problems, although it did lead to a little excitement today. Geronimo Hernandez (Sr.) owns girls house but lives half-way to Quimistan with family because it is closer to his field. He seldom in town during the week, but he came to look us over this afternoon and was so pleased by the improvements to his house that he told Sue that he wanted to give us some fresh meat. She became agitated and came running over saying, "They're going to kill the bull for us." Juan quickly got clarification that the offering was a chicken for dinner.

Dinner was a feast with the boiled chicken plus homemade bread courtesy of Don Pedro's family supplementing our rice and beans.

Unfortunately, I'm not over the illness. I had to beat a hasty retreat to the edge of the ravine to in time for my stomach to empty.

After dinner, Juan, Doug and Ed left for Quimistan for mail, a little shopping, and probably for some *Nacional* beer. Meanwhile, the girls started a game of *Loteria* (similar to Bingo) in the school. The party at the school broke up early (around 7:30) because of impending rain. One of the schoolboys, Nico, followed me back to my cot and said he was worried about me. I told him I'll be all right soon. He stayed an extra half-hour talking. His show of concern definitely helped me feel better, as well as taking my mind off my stomach. He hopes to be a teacher when he grows up.

We thought the gringo watching was slowing down, but apparently they were just saving their steam for tonight. I think they are getting more accustomed to us, however. The women are freer in talking with us and they are completely baffled by our girls' working on our projects. (The social situation has taught them that physical labor is not part of their place and they really think it is beyond their capability.)

Hopefully, tomorrow we finish working for ourselves and the owners of the two houses. I'm afraid we have spent a lot of unnecessary work and time on them which could have been put to better use. I hope that we haven't given townsfolk the impression that their homes aren't good enough for us. We sure don't want to increase the amount of jealousy in the village. The one advantage the work has had is it gave us something to do immediately on arrival so we didn't have the embarrassing waiting period which plagued some teams in the prior years.

The bug swatting is getting bad so the hour must be late.

Sunday, July 4

Fourth of July in Honduras is really no different from the third, or the fifth for that matter, which is when I'm writing this, Sunday having been a big day for all of us.

Sunday is a day of rest. For the locals, that means no work in the fields – but collecting wood for cooking is common. Some listen to a Mass on the radio.

For our part, we chose to be slothful by setting the alarm clock for 6:00am instead of our accustomed 5:30. By the time we got moving, some kids were playing/washing their hands at the pipe in our backyard. They seemed to love the chance to use soap. I was still feeling a little weak, but the oatmeal breakfast filled my stomach and had me feeling better.

The carpenter and Don Antonio showed up before 7:00, I think. They were rewarded for the Sunday morning promptness with Don Lelo's ranting and raving about precisely where, give or take eight centimeters, the *lavarastes* (outdoor table for the laundry tub) which the girls never wanted in the first place, was to be built. As much help as Don Lelo has given us, I think it is time for him to move on. The goodwill of the community is one of the most valuable things we have; I hope no one is irked by the occasional lack of communication we are beset by.

Work virtually stopped, to no one's surprise, when Rafael Davila arrived in his privately hired VW taxi. It was good he came, nonetheless, because as a Rotarian he can now report to the club members on our progress and projected plans. He looked over the school site and discussed the *comedor* requirements. He promised to return next Sunday with engineering diagrams for its construction.

Let's hope more personal, as well as financial aid is forthcoming from our benefactors. Don Lelo has once more said it was about time for him to leave. This time his departure is slated for Monday morning. He has contacts to make in San Pedro, and although not himself a Rotarian, has the influence we need to keep the Milparada project a going concern.

We finally gave the houses a final sweeping and in a great community campaign, moved our baggage, cots and field kitchen into our new houses. A house is not, as they say, a home, but that holds only if one WANTS a home. While we boys pretty much just shoved our personal stuff in the back room and set the tools and materials against the walls of the front room, our girls did a much nicer job of arranging things in their house. By their own admission, they feel like they're playing house, but it's satisfying to see them making a home in what is surely their first own house.

The housewarming dinner-by-candlelight was simple, pretty and delicious. I hope they know how much the boys appreciate their efforts.

The town's traditional and customary Saturday evening dance was postponed a day till the gringos moved out of the schoolhouse, which serves as the dance hall. The whole affair was in our honor, by which is meant that the scores of townsfolk who turned out wanted us to show how we dance (*a la Americana*) while they stand and watch. And so they did – seven people deep, grinning from ear to ear. They loved it. Things got a little tense at first when we made Pedro understand that we'd like everyone to dance, but as the ballroom gradually filled with gliding couples, the anxiety eased, and even Melissa stopped shaking and enjoyed a room-temperature Coke with the boys. A seemingly simple incident, the offering of beer and Coke and chicklets, but it was the best they had to give us. There are a lot of things we receive differently as we realize the sacrifice being made to give them. In a like manner, we will grow in our appreciation of both what we have and what we can give.

I sat out the most of the dancing, pleading that I was still a little under the weather. The truth of the matter is that I'm not much of a dancer and felt quite embarrassed by having so many people watching my version of the twist.

During the dance, I had a long talk with the male school teacher, *Profesor* Jacobo. Once I told him that I planned to become a mathematics teacher after I finish college, he spoke very openly. *Profesor* Jacobo is close to my age. He arrived in Milparada one month before we did – fresh from completing three years at the Technical School in Tegucigalpa. That means he has had a total of nine years of schooling. He is proud of being progressive. He makes L120 (sixty dollars) a month and pays L23 for food to a lady in town. He lives alone, rent free. He tells me that he plays the guitar (but doesn't own one). He clearly likes the kids and seems to generally intelligent and committed to his profession. He prefers first grade (telling me that it is the "most important") and working with poorer people. He is concerned that the people with money are wasteful, "You should be careful to fully use everything." As an example, he showed me one of the CARE desks and suggested changing the design to use less wood. (His suggested change would make them less sturdy.) Nevertheless, he is applying for a job with United Fruit Company. ("They pay much more than the government.")

Jacobo is extremely eager to learn English, to the point of being a nuisance. He always carries some beat up paper with him with some English words on it. He had taken a correspondence course in English so he knows a few words - "Come down; I am your friend, said the little cat." He's the one who made the sign that greeted us on the school house door: "You are welcome / or don't mention it / Open the door said the little mouse."

Teachers employed by national government earn *L*90 to *L*200 per month, paid for twelve months, including the school vacation from December to February. The pay depends on the amount of education and whether it is a rural or urban assignment. The number of years of experience doesn't make a difference. Urban teachers require at least four years of *colegio* after sixth grade, with pay starting at *L*150. Rural teachers need only to have completed sixth grade. There is no concept of tenure, but Jacobo is not worried about keeping a job because there is a shortage of teachers, especially for the rural areas. Teaching assignments are for one year, but a teacher can usually stay on if both the teacher and the head of the school desire it.

The students normally start first grade between the ages of seven and nine. Seven is the minimum age for government school. The students need to supply their own pencil and writing paper. Government schooling is free through age fifteen or sixth grade, whichever comes first. It takes an average of four years to complete primary school (through third grade). Many of the children repeat first grade. For every grade, Final Examinations are held for three days in November. Teachers switch schools to administer the exams, to make sure they don't let the students cheat. This one set of examinations covers all materials for each grade level and result in grades of Failed, Passed, or Distinguished for each student. A student needs to get a "Distinguished" grade on the third grade exam to be eligible for continued education. Last year half of the students in Milparada passed. Five got Distinguished marks.

The current Milparada schoolhouse had been started by a progressive teacher four years ago. But he got recalled for more training, so the incomplete building with foundation and walls but no floor or roof sat empty while classes continued to be held in the old one-room mud hut. The next year, Milparada got a bad teacher. None of the twenty-four students passed any grade test. His replacement only lasted a couple of years. She was an outspoken Liberal, and when the Nationalists took over the government, she was replaced for political reasons. Dona Florifilia was the teacher last year when Don Lelo and the Cornell team in Quimistan got the new school completed. She still lives in Milparada, in a whitewashed wood house with painted trim and the only vegetable garden in town. She was raised in San Pedro and now runs a small store out of her house.

The whole town is very proud of the new school and of their children being able to read. Enrollment jumped to fifty-four students this year, compared to thirty-two the previous year. Even with this increase, and the availability of a two-room schoolhouse, Milparada started the year with only one teacher.

Profesora Maria Luisa appears to be in her late thirties and is in charge of the school. She is a traditionalist. To her, the purpose of school is to teach literacy and promote a sense of national citizenship. She expresses a strong interest in English, but doesn't care for mathematics. I think she is not particularly bright. She shows little interest in the kids; she is a teacher because it is the best job she could get.

School is held Monday through Friday, plus Saturday morning. Jacobo invited me to visit the school tomorrow. That should be very interesting. The official schedule is posted in large lettering on the front wall of the school room:

7:50	Attendance
8:00	Reading
9:00	Recreation
9:20	Mathematics: Monday, Tuesday, Thursday, Friday
	Health: Wednesday
	Reading: Saturday
10:20	Drawing: Monday & Thursday
	Music: Tuesday & Friday
	Art: Wednesday & Saturday
10:50	Lunch Recess
1:50	Attendance
2:00	Reading: Tuesday & Thursday
	Writing: Monday, Wednesday, Friday
2:30	Natural Science: two days
	Social Studies: three days
3:10	Recreation
3:20	Agriculture: three days
	Industrial Arts and Home Economics: 2 days
4:00	General assembly
4:10	dismissal

At the end of the dance, the townspeople insisted that I sing for them with my guitar. My new version of "This Land" was an instant hit:

Esta tierra es tuya,

This land is your land,

Esta tierra es mia,

This land is my land,

De los Estados Unidos

From the United States

hasta Honduras,

to Honduras

De las ciudades grandes

From the big cities

a los pueblos pequenos,

to the small villages,

Esta tierra se hizo para mi y para ti.

This land was made for you and me.

1. Es Milparada
Mi pueblo amado,

Milparada is
my beloved town,

Donde cada uno es amigo

Where each person is a friend

de cada otro;

of everyone else;

Donde los de Cornell viven

Where the Cornell students live

Con sus hermanos Honduranos en

with their Honduran brothers in

esta tierra que se hizo para mi y ti

This land that was made for your & me.

2. Somos todos ciudanos

We are all citizens

de las Americas nuestras

of our Americas.

En mucho somos similares

We have much in common

aunque parecemos diferentes.

although we appear to be different.

Podemos ayudarnos,

We can help ourselves,

Cada uno a los otros, en

Each aiding the others, in

esta tierra que se hizo para mi y ti
me.

This land that was made for your & me.

Monday, July 5

Today was, we could say, a slow day. Don Lelo left and it was somewhat of a relief. We don't have any physical work to do today. Now that we are moved into our houses, we have set up a rotating schedule for cooking. Two of us will be handling the kitchen duties each day, switching the pairings after each four days. Fixing breakfast is easy. Our standard breakfast has become a large bowl of oatmeal, with a little powdered milk and sugar, plus coffee. A couple of times a week, we are able to buy enough eggs to add fried or scrambled eggs to the menu.

The main goal for today is to start our literacy program. Most of the team members will be going around town and talking with people to spread the news and encourage participation. That left me free to take up *Profesor* Jacobo's invitation.

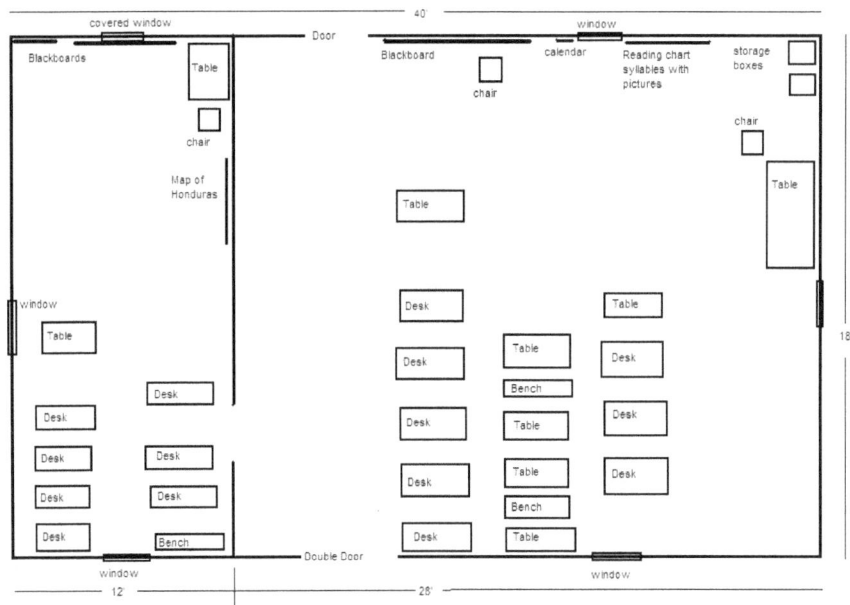

Figure 2. School floor plan

I went into the school early and made a map of the facility. The need for more desks was apparent. Half of the kids are now stuck sitting on rickety benches behind small tables that are too tall for them to comfortably write on. The main room has one battered blackboard, a pretty print of the Honduran coat of arms and flag, various charts and vocabulary lists that have been hand printed by the teachers, and two boxes containing a few books. The third grade classroom has two blackboards and a tattered wall map of Honduras. Each room has a small table and chair for the teacher. The teacher's table had a twelve-inch ruler, a couple of books, a little paper, and six pieces of chalk.

When *Profesora* Maria Luisa came in, she asked me to bring my guitar so we could start the day with "*Tu Bandera*" (Your Flag), the national anthem - So much for sitting inconspicuously in the back of the room and observing.

The kids gathered outside, until the teacher called them in for attendance. There is no clock in the school and neither teacher has a watch. Nevertheless school started only five minutes late and all day stayed within fifteen or twenty minutes of the schedule. I'm impressed.

The class started with roll call. The children address the teachers as *Profesora* and *Profesor*, no names. Attendance for the third grade is nine boys and five girls, with two absent girls. For the combined first and second grade class, twelve girls and sixteen boys answer the call, so only twenty-six of the thirty-eight registered students are here. I don't know if the high number of absences is normal, or a result of the chicken pox epidemic. One more small boy came in as we were finishing the national anthem. *Profesor* Jacobo instructed him, "Go to the river for a bath." I'm not sure whether that was a punishment or a reflection on the child's cleanliness. He definitely wasn't the only boy with a dirty face.

I observed the second graders as they moved into the third grade room for reading. The main difference between their materials is that the reading book for second grade has bigger type. There are textbooks for all subjects in all grades. The Milparada school has only one copy of each text. The teacher uses it for lectures. New material is introduced by a lecture out of text book and a command to "copy from the blackboard." The kids take turns taking a book home to study. (If that child is absent the next day, then there will be no lecture in that subject.)

The first grade reading involved reciting the alphabet and phonetically sounding out single words. The teachers carry a leather strap or small slap-stick to keep order during the boring classes. When the *Profesor* stepped into the other room to talk with the other teacher, thirteen of the first graders got out of their seats. When he came back he lined them all up and whipped each one in the small of the back (boys and girls equally). The other common punishment is being kept inside during recess for a stern lecture on how they should behave.

When recreation time was announced, the children ran out, screaming to each other. The boys played a vicious style of soccer, basically pushing each other away from the ball. I didn't see any voluntary passing. The girls had been taught a few games by past teachers, but for the most part were accustomed to unsupervised, individual scampers. I hadn't placed much importance on our plans for running a recreation program, but this display of near chaos shows that there may be some real value to establishing some sort of organized sports and games. Maybe a program could increase the children's sense of cooperation and sportsmanship while providing constructive exercise.

When we went back inside for mathematics, *Profesor* Jacobo had the first and second grade students arranged in three groups. Group A is for independent workers: ten girls and two boys. Group B is for normal learners: two girls and eight boys. Group C is for the students who are behind in their learning: all seven in this group are boys.

He started class with the following problems on the board for the A's to copy and solve:

32 cows -	62 dogs -	72 hogs -	32 oxen
—			
18 cows	49 dogs	67 hogs	16 oxen

The teacher spent most of his time addressing group B, leaving the C's in the back of the room to follow along the best they can. The kids respond to his questions as a chorus of voices. He started by holding up two small rocks.

"What are these?"

Chorus: "Rocks"

"What color are they?"

Chorus: "White"

"Where do we find these white rocks?"

The chorus had a variety of answers, at least one including the word "river"

"Correct. We find this kind of white rock only in the river. How many rocks do I have here?"

Chorus: "Two"

"If I take one away, how many do I have left?"

Chorus: "One"

The teacher continued in this manner for both addition and subtraction – holding rocks, matchboxes, or bottle tops in his hands. Then he made the arithmetic operations more explicit:

"If I have four little boxes (in one hand) and a child gives me three more (holds them up in the other hand), how many boxes do I have (hands are together)?"

Chorus: "Seven"

"Four and three are?"

Chorus: "Seven"

(He puts his hands behind his back.) "Four plus three are?"

Chorus: "Seven"

The boys in group C are watching pretty attentively, but are quiet. The B's are excited and shouting out the answers. When the teacher hears a wrong answer, he has that student count the objects to get the correct responses. His tone of voice in making corrections is gentle.

This lecture lasts about fifteen minutes. Before it is over, all of the A's are finished with their problems. Most of the girls were sewing and talking. The boys were standing around talking. The teacher ignored them and went to the right-side of the blackboard, which has rows of different shapes on it – such as

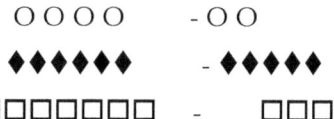

"Here are four circles" – Everyone counts them aloud.

"Minus two circles" – Everyone counts, "One, two."

"If I take two circles away from four (crosses out two of the circles), how many do I have left?" The chorus replies "Two"

He writes: 4 -   "Four minus two are?" Chorus: "Two"

                      2

He writes   2

This sequence is repeated for each row. (I am surprised to see that the minus sign is written after the number on the top line, instead of in front of the bottom number.)

Next he erased the board and wrote a set of twelve single-digit subtraction problems, announcing that it is time for independent work. He loaned a small pile of rocks to two students (who just started school this month). Another boy asked for rocks.

"You don't need them. You know enough to work alone."

While they were working, he went over and corrected the A's papers, explaining how to fix the errors. He wrote eight more subtraction problems on their side of the board.

Returning to the B and C groups, he corrected their papers, having them count matchboxes to revise wrong answers. This math class ran considerably longer than the official schedule. It is now 10:30, leaving a short time for the Drawing class. That class consisted of the teacher making a crude sketch on the board and having all of the kids copy it.

The lunch break is nearly two hours. That allows the children enough time to do household chores. I chose to spend the afternoon in the other room, observing the other teacher. The curriculum did not match the posted schedule. Starting at 1:55 pm, the second and third graders were together for a science test. The students had to copy each sentence from the board (so I guess this could count as the writing lesson), and mark it as either True or False. The questions were on one of the blackboards:

1. The heart is an organ of the digestive system.
2. The lungs are enveloped in a membrane called pleura.
3. Ornamental plants are used for medicine.
4. A seed needs heat, water and sun to germinate.
5. The digestive system is made up of the stomach, veins and lungs.
6. The upper arm bone is called the humerus.
7. The sense of taste is for seeing.
8. A flower is made of roots, stem and leaves.
9. Water in its solid state is found in the river.
10. Sand and asbestos form plaster
11. Sugar cane and tobacco are industrial plants

After fifteen minutes, she collected all their papers and gave the answers. The passing grade for such tests is fifty percent correct.

The second graders went back to the large room (carrying their desks), while the third graders stay for Social Studies. *Profesora* Maria Luisa has the larger blackboards covered with questions and calls on individual kids who have their hands raised to answer. However, the answers are shouted out in chorus, so it is almost impossible to me to distinguish specific answers in the hubbub. The words in parentheses are my notes.

1. Where is Honduras situated? (Central America)
2. How many Departments (provinces) does Honduras have?
3. What is the capital of Honduras?
4. Name the boundaries of Honduras.
5. Why is the land of Honduras broken up? (The correct answer is "Because there are many mountains.")
6. What is the perimeter of Honduras? (Answer to the nearest kilometer)
7. What races exist in Honduras? (Whites, Indians, Blacks, Yellow and *Mestizos*)

8. What are our Indians like? (Accepted answer: They all live on the Mosquito Coast – which is inaccurate)
9. Who discovered Central America?
10. Who were the conquerors of Honduras?
11. Where was Limpira (early Indian resistance leader) from?
12. Where was El Sabio Valle (the man who wrote the charter of Independence for Central America) born?
13. What did they call Jose Trinidad Cabenas?
14. What were the works written by Padre Reyes?
15. With what Republic does Honduras have boundaries?
16. What is the major Pacific port?
17. What is the name of the island province of Honduras?
18. Name the capital of the Department of Intibucir?
19. How is a Department formed? (Something about an area with more than 10,000 people)
20. How many municipalities are in the Department of Santa Barbara? ("There are twenty-six. Name some of them" : Quimistan, San Marcos and two others mentioned)
21. Name the National symbols? (Flag, Coat of Arms, Pine tree, Flower, Bird)
22. What are the methods of communication in Honduras? (Telegraph, car, mail, telephone …)
23. Who wrote the National Anthem?
24. What are the sections of a home? (bedroom, dining room, kitchen – The teacher added, "Sanitation facilities, which we don't have here.")
25. Who is the main authority in a village?" (Auxiliary Mayor – Teacher adds "In school, the Master is the top authority. What's the name of Milparada's Auxiliary Mayor?" – Taurino. "His last name?" None of the children knows, so the teacher explains the importance of a last name particularly if you are trying to find somebody in San Pedro Sula.)
26. What does the Department of Santa Barbara produce? (The kids answered, "Corn, beans." The teacher noted, "Those are produced all over, but each department produces different things like bananas. What special things does Santa Barbara produce?" "Palm fiber, cattle, horses and coffee." "Yes, Santa Barbara is the biggest producer of coffee.")
27. What does the equilateral triangle on the Honduras Coat of Arms stand for? (This drew noise as a response. The teacher clarified: "The three rights of man: Liberty, Fraternity and Equality. They came from the French Revolution. Ricardo – do you know when the French Revolution was?" Several boys

answer "1787." "Yes, starting with Bastille Day on the 14th of July, 1787"

The official Writing lesson started at 2:45. The students are sent to the board one at a time to write a sentence (in script) from the teacher's dictation. The sentences come from an article about Honduras. The sentence is repeated word by word. While one student is writing, the rest of the boys are chatting or looking out the window and most of the girls continue to sew. When the student finishes, everyone points out the errors. The most common errors are near miss phonetics ("v" for "b"; "z" for "s") or mistakes in capitalization.

Profesora Maria Luisa's main technique in correcting errors is embarrassment. The kids almost always come back from the board looking dejected. But there are still lots of volunteers wanting to answer each question. She talks almost constantly with the same (rather sharp) tone of voice whether scolding ("Victoriano, there is no reason to look out the window when there is nothing in the street."), asking a question, or making an observation or explanation.

Before the afternoon recess, the teacher wrote the third grade math homework assignment on the board. Only five out of the fourteen students copied it down.)

T	qq	@	lb	onz	
7	18	95	70	92	+
9	73	65	86	96	

(T =tons; qq = quintals, a 100 pound unit; @ = arrobas a 25 pound unit, lb=pounds, onz=ounces. The instruction is to add and reduce.)

$$\frac{180}{5} \ X \ \frac{7}{2} \ X \ \frac{150}{3} \ =$$

$$6862 -$$
$$4989$$

$$86,753 / 9$$

$$37,576 \ x \ 54 =$$

The afternoon recess was a repeat of the morning's activity.

From 4:00 to4:30, the third grade had a science lesson. The questions were read by the teacher (nothing was on the board this time). The answers again came in the form of an uncoordinated chorus, out of which the teacher selected, or created, the correct answer. The lesson covered questions on different areas of science in a seeming random order:

"What are the three parts of the body?" "Head, trunk, extremities."

"What is air made of?" "Twenty-one parts oxygen, seventy-six parts nitrogen, one part water and one part dissolved particles."

"What is moving air called?" "Wind."

"What is an organism?" "An organism is something which is born, grows, reproduces and has organs."

"How do bees make honey?" "They fly from the hive, get nectar and pollen from flowers and make honey from them."

"Name the five parts of a tree." "Roots, leaves, flowers, fruit and trunk."

"For germination, seeds need air, heat and humidity." (Then the teacher added, " And not to have lost the power of germination by being left in a very hot place.")

"Name some monochotic plants" "Corn, mangos."

"Some dichotic?" "Rose"

"What are the 5 senses?" "Taste, touch, vision, smell, hearing."

"What is sand?" (The teacher's answer: "Sand is a heavy grey mineral which is not soluble in water.")

"Water exists in three states: liquid, solid and gaseous."

"What does air serve for?" "It is for us to breathe. It makes the sky blue. The wind brings rain, and air transports sound."

After school was dismissed, I asked some of the boys if they liked school. (The girls went straight to their homes, while most of the boys hung out around the plaza.) They were unanimous in expressing a desire to learn. When I asked specifically how they could use the things they learned in school, the only answer was that they could read the signs in the stores. They didn't believe that school would change what they did later in life; they all expect to work in the fields after third grade.

Overall, the day's experience left me feeling sad - all of that enthusiasm, energy and ability, and no prospect for a better future. The schooling provides little more than rote learning of set answers to unrelated questions. Other than the first grade math class, there was no hands-on involvement or demonstrations. I'm probably being too harsh in my judgments. I doubt I could do much better with only the materials available in this school. I can't help but compare these boys to their age-mates back home. In the United States, the eleven to fourteen year olds would be in junior high instead of just third grade. It is hard for me to imagine boys going into the work force right after third grade.

I passed my own "Spanish test." I was able to keep up and understand everything the teachers said – better yet, I realize that I was comprehending and taking notes without consciously translating the words into English. A full week of total immersion has greatly improved my fluency.

In the afternoon, we had a very disturbing experience. A man came to see if we could help his wife who had been bleeding from four teeth she pulled out one week ago. She had been bleeding since early morning and came to see Melissa at about 5:30pm. Fortunately a man from *Banco Internacional de Desarrollo* (International Bank of Development) was visiting us and he drove her to Quimistan to see a doctor.

We started our literacy program this evening. We will be holding classes three times a week. A number of the village teens and men showed up wanting to learn English! *Profesora* Maria Luisa was the only woman to show up. We did have seven actual literacy students. Two of them, Antonio and another man, could read but came to learn how to sign their names. So, the other five got individual tutoring using the *Alfalit* pamphlets. I was matched with a teenager, Juan Ramon. At the start, he didn't even know the alphabet. I was pleasantly surprised at how easy the materials were to use. I followed the instructions specifically, working with pictures of familiar objects starting with the same letter to create an association between the letter and a phonetic sound, and providing lots of encouragement. I'm glad that Spanish uses such consistent pronunciation and spelling. I would hate to try to do the same thing with our convoluted English language. At the end of our half-hour session, both Juan Ramon and I were proud of his progress.

We had wondered about the value of an eight week course in the very basics of the language and had debated the necessity and purpose for holding such a class. But, based on tonight's response, we have no choice. Sue had a dozen enthusiastic and excited students.

At our nightly meeting Sue reported on her experience with the English program – given the size of that class some of the rest of us are likely to need to step in. She had found no book that was absolutely basic enough for such a short term project, so she used the blackboard and the students copied from it. We would teach important phrases (greetings, weather, requests) and pertinent words and numbers. Her preparatory research indicates that it is better to teach by identification, rather than translation. Instead of asking, "How do you say *casa*?" She would point at a house and let them make their own transposition. The method is basically: listen, imitate, repeat. Listen, imitate, repeat. We will do a lot of review, rehashing all of the phrases from the previous class. The rationale being that if they were going to receive any satisfaction from the classes, it would come from being able to say a few things well.

Admittedly, there is the fault that they will probably never use their few acquired English phrases; they hold only short term prestige value. I suppose every single one of the students, in a far off dream, would want to come to the United States. Therefore, they want to learn English. We and they knew that this wasn't a possibility. But by teaching English, we were able to encourage an intellectual path into a new world, into a new knowledge.

In any case, the classes give us a way to meet more people and to work with them on an equal basis. For they know that while we were teaching English or literacy, they know that we were working on improving our Spanish, and they are helping us with that. The classes are also a way to repay the villagers, to thank them for cooperating with us, providing us with housing, and making us feel comfortable.

We are all learning. At least we are clearly seeing how large the problems are here.

Tuesday, July 6

Our team was short-staffed today. Melissa was on an excursion giving vaccinations in San Marcos and Juan and Doug have gone into San Pedro doing errands (among other things). The early morning wake-up and tediousness of the bus ride are offset by the prospect of hot showers and cold beers.

Our nurses are very busy. The chickenpox is calming down, but in addition to all types of miscellaneous wounds and sickness, a lot of kids are coming down with pink eye. Also, about half the kids have intestinal worms. Unfortunately, we don't have any medicines that will treat that problem.

The first week of our stay in Milparada, the people were naturally shy and did not really know our function. Perhaps news spread of our medical equipment as a result of Soila, a young girl who had cut her foot badly on a rock. Noting the dirty rag tied around her foot, we offered to bandage it and she agreed. She returned every day for a week or more for dressing changes.

After that start, patients sprang up rapidly – women with breast abscesses, children with chicken pox (then in epidemic form in the village), pregnant women with swollen legs, children with minor eye infections resulting from the small flies always at their eyes, etc. And again as word spread of our medicine, each day ten or twelve persons (some women with their infants) would come to the house for medicine (and some "gringo watching" to be sure). The medicine we had consisted of cough medicine, antibiotic ointments, penicillin for injection and in tablet form, eye and nose drops, gentian violet, iodine, alcohol, some vitamins, grippe pills, and of course aspirin. Most of these medicines as well as some of our bandage supply were gifts from members of the San Pedro Rotary Club.

The most common maladies sprang from the living conditions. Small gnats caused eye infections, impure water and food, intestinal parasites and diarrhea, poor nutrition, weakness, muscle and joint pains, temperatures, machete wounds, uncleanliness, abscesses and boils. It was, of course, possible to give the people eye drops, but the gnats would come again; Kaopectate, but the impure food, etc. would be eaten again; vitamins, but they would be used up and the pains would come again; bandages, but they would get cut again.

The mystery is not to see the people coming daily for medicine, but to wonder what they do when no nurse or doctor is available. There is a nurse in Quimistan, but she won't practice outside the walls of the clinic. (Maybe she is required to stay on site to protect the medical supplies.) On

Tuesdays, each week, the Alliance for Progress doctor holds a clinic in Quimistan. However, Quimistan is about an hour's walk for these people who have no car at all and the fifty-cent charge at the clinic is beyond most of the villagers' pocketbook.

It is no wonder that the people mostly rely on their folk medicines. Their medicine? They have a sort of preparation which is used as an all-purpose applicant – rubbed into wounds and sore areas. Aspirin are not unknown, but they cost money. There is a type of bug which is supposedly remedial for ear trouble when dried and crushed into a powder. The sap from one plant is good for relieving pain from bug-bite itches and burns. (I tried that one on some of my bites, and it does work.) Still farther from the realm of the twentieth century is a remedy for fever: Open a pigeon from sternum to tail after twisting off the head, then place the open pigeon over the arms of the patient.

The task of seeking medical change here would seem insurmountable. Yet, when we see a mal-nourished baby crying for more of a bitter medicine from the doctor which a well fed baby would spit out, we know we must make our best effort.

About 10:00, two very clean-cut Honduran young men appeared in a blue jeep – Charlie and Guillermo. They are representatives from the Alliance for Progress working in the Quimistan District. They had met Melissa this morning and came to offer us any help they could, saying they would help build latrines or drive us anywhere. The Alliance for Progress team is funded to help outlying towns with health and sanitation. While associated with the regional clinic, Charlie and Guillermo generally function independently, organizing latrine building programs, vaccination clinics and giving health classes (with the aid of puppets). This is their first visit to Milparada. Since our team has set an example with the only latrine in Milparada, they would like to use that as leverage for starting a village-wide latrine construction program later in the summer.

I asked about the water supply. They said we are very lucky in that regard. Milparada is one of the few places in Honduras where the water is safe to drink. It is piped directly from mountain springs. (Nevertheless, at dinner tonight our team decided to continue our regime of boiling water, just to stay on the safe side.) On the other hand, the river water is contaminated by the cattle grazing up stream, rotting vegetation and a variety of other pollutants.

They also gave us the low down on the resident "doctor" we had met in Quimistan. He is generally respected by the *campesinos*, including Antonio Machado. He had told us he was losing a lot of patients with cholera. ("Two or three days and you're gone.") Guillermo assures us that there hasn't been a single case of cholera in years in the entire North Coast region. These cases are most likely simple cases of gastorentesitis. The self-proclaimed doctor has also given false reports of malaria.

He doesn't have any college degree. His only medical training came as part of his past job as a lab technician for the United Fruit Company. His wife serves as his nurse, but she has no training at all. They make a good living off of poor farmers, especially on illegal abortions. (When he can't stop the bleeding from resulting hemorrhage, he sends the patient to the Alliance Doctor with instructions to tell him "I fell.")

In conclusion we learned that they don't have the equipment, facilities or knowledge to deal with some of the more serious medical problems. Nevertheless, until the Alliance opened their clinic, he was the only source of care in the immediate area.

I spent some more time in the school today. The third grade math lesson covered "multiplying fractions." However, when teacher demonstrated how to work a problem, she actually went through the steps for adding fractions. (Juan of our team said his elementary teacher in Costa Rica taught him the same mistake.) Third grade mathematics also includes multiplying by two digits, long division, along with conversions using a variety of units of weight, length and time. Most of the class time is spent with one student at a time working a problem on the blackboard. Nico eagerly volunteered for the first problem, but needed lots of prodding and correcting to complete it. The teacher struggled with her own arithmetic calculations. She is no more fluent in multiplication tables than the kids.

Profesor Jacobo entered the room in middle of this lesson and both teachers start practicing their new English on me. While this is going on, two of the boys walked up to the board to help and correct the girl who was standing at the board. When Jacobo left, *Profesora* Maria Luisa bawled out Victor for not having his homework. I don't know why he was singled out. The majority of the students did not have any written problems with them. She then called Victor up and gave him a new problem for adding different weight units. When he started to write out the conversions as division problems, the teacher stopped him and insisted he do it all mentally.

At 2:00, it was time for Industrial Arts and Home Economics. That curriculum turns out to be basket weaving for the boys and sewing/embroidery for the girls. *Profesora* Maria spent the hour outside helping some boys with basket weaving. Three boys were actually working on baskets, two others were watching, the rest just hung around). *Profesor* Jacobo stayed inside making a basket for an audience of two first grade boys. Many of the girls stayed at their desks sewing on their own. While the basket work was very coarse, the girls' embroidery looked very good. About half the students were no place to be seen.

About 4:30 pm a hysterical woman came running up to our house cradling a toddler. She was sobbing, "My son is ruined. He will never be a man. He has cut his male parts. I fear he will die." We were only partially successful in calming her down while Mary examined the boy. Sue grabbed the bicycle and rode off to fetch Charlie and Guillermo. The boy had been wandering around his house when he grabbed a machete and tripped with it between his legs. It made a large gash, which actually was on the thigh side of his groin. I could see the tendon, but it wasn't severed. There was surprisingly little blood. Mary cleaned the wound and applied a compression bandage. Charlie drove up within the hour and took the mother and child to the clinic. We were doubly lucky, having just met Charlie and Guillermo and having the accident on a Tuesday – the only day the real doctor visits Quimistan. This incident really made our isolation hit home.

Melissa got back in time for dinner and gave us an account of her trip to San Marcos. She went by horseback from Quimistan, following a path through the hills. Her job today was to start the *Amigos de Honduras* in Quimistan on their vaccination program by okaying their techniques. The *Amigos* is an organization based in Houston that recruited doctors and teenagers (mostly high school seniors) from churches for three-week tours to give immunizations to the poor.

The Amigos are here in the noblest of spirits – but the first year of their program is off to a slow beginning. Their objective is wholesale inoculations (DPT, polio and small pox). They got off to a bad start. Their medicines didn't arrive until two weeks after the first group of volunteers. Since few of them spoke any Spanish, they were stuck just hanging around fighting boredom with each other. They were also poorly trained. When vaccines finally arrived, they started shooting indiscriminately – a lot of bad reactions resulted from vaccinating currently sick people. The Ministry of Health started to shut them down, but reached a compromise for the next cycles by adding two local representatives from the San Pedro Health Center to each team – to screen out inappropriate clients. The other big problem was that they targeted many of the same towns as the Alliance health team. So, in San Marcos only thirty out of the population of three thousand got the DPT shots from the *Amigos*.

In fairness, Melissa said they had an excellent technique executing the campaign against smallpox and TB. On the day the vaccinating team was to arrive, a loudspeaker truck came and drove throughout the town blaring forth a warning against the two dreaded diseases and offering the free vaccine. The Health Center representative went into the school and explained the two vaccines to the children. He told them that surely if they saw a poisonous snake, they would use their machete to kill it, and just so, these vaccines would be machetes in their bodies to kill the harmful diseases.

The vaccinations themselves were performed with the new high-speed "Pistol of Peace," which is so rapid that two hundred persons can be vaccinated in an hour. Furthermore, the technique is sterile. The standard procedure of the Alliance nurses for DPT is not-antiseptic: one disposable syringe was used for two children, the needle being wiped with alcohol between uses.

In return for Melissa's help, the "Amigos de Honduras" will be making a visit to Milparada to give vaccinations for smallpox and injections of BCG against tuberculosis.

This evening we played lottery played with corn cob kernels by candlelight, using pieces of hard candy as prizes. Pedro, Irma, Juan, various relations, neighbors, friends and gringos played. The game is simple enough, but important in that we were all playing together – united in fun.

Ten days in town – we are becoming more settled, more accepted and fitting in somewhat – now that we are in our permanent quarters, they always know where they can go "gringo watch." More mothers are coming for help, more just to talk and visit. They enjoy seeing us trying to cook over our wood stove. (We have converted from the costlier kerosene burners, partly because of the cost and partly because the size of the stove top makes it easier to handle multiple pots.) The women are always ready to offer the girls suggestions about recipes, and local remedies (bug salves, sun burn ointments and witch doctor chants). Yes – this is a poor town, but it is rich in warmth and sharing.

Wednesday, July 7

Doug and Juan didn't return last night.

Today was somewhat of a restful day topped with some pleasant surprises. Trinchi cooked breakfast, oatmeal plus *pan dulce* (sweet rolls) – a gift from Don Lelo. I enlisted the help of some of the boys, who were hanging out before school, to put up the volleyball posts and nets. When school started, I set about clearing the volleyball court with my machete. That task was hard on my back, but I preferred it to the alternative of washing clothes in the backyard. I dealt with the heat by taking some drinks directly from the water tap in the plaza. The fresh water is cooler and more refreshing than our boiled supply, and I've had no ill effects.

During recreation hour, I supervised the boys' soccer game, having limited success in convincing the boys to pass the ball. Meanwhile Mary, Sue, Trinchi and *Profesor* Jacobo played volleyball with the girls. It appears that the children are unaccustomed to batting a ball and kept catching it to throw back over the net. We may have to play as a team to demonstrate as well as "recreate."

Our designated helper for today was Luis Hernan Castillo. He owns the best oxcart in town (which just means that it is better than Antonio's). So I took advantage of that to gather sand for mixing cement for the *comedor's* foundation and floor. Luis has a reputation for being a loafer. He spent a fair amount of time watching us last week, but hasn't helped out until today. He arrived with a teenaged assistant, Antonio, who may be his son. Antonio is deaf, but does speak in a manner that Luis can understand. Antonio is rather clumsy with his hands, but he is good at soccer and is a regular participant in the late afternoon games. I have seen no sign of there being any stigma attached to his handicap. During our return trip with the first load of sand, Luis told me that "Mexico and Central America are the only places still using oxcarts, even Cuba now uses tractors and trucks." Because of this he admires Cuba. This is the first positive thing I have heard about Castro since we arrived in Honduras. Luis is a native of Milparada, so he has inherited some of the better growing land. He may be the most educated native of the village, having attended public *colegio* in San Pedro for two years after completing sixth grade. He speaks a little English and told me that he has two books on English which he studies.

Nelly Duarte's yellow truck appeared in the middle of the morning with Nelly and Chito, her helper. It was laden with coconuts, plantains, fresh cream, pineapples, cookies, magazines, and canned peaches. What a friend! Nelly stayed for our lunch (by Sue and Ed) speaking very well in English.

Jacobo talked about his plans to make a school vegetable garden. It would serve as the Agriculture class and could add fresh vegetables to the *comedor* meals. The children would do all the work. We eagerly agreed that this would be a great addition to the projects that we had planned. Guillermo had told him that he could get free seeds from the Alliance for Progress, so the biggest problem would be getting enough wood for a fence to keep the animals, including chickens and rabbits, from eating the crops. Nelly said she knows the owner of a sawmill in Cordaderos and insisted on driving some of us there to get scrap wood. I volunteered nails and the use of our tools.

The round trip to the sawmill only took about two hours. We came back with a full load of six and eight foot pieces of wood from the rounded edges of logs, more than adequate for our needs. I was surprised to see a large termite nest in a tree on the edge of the sawmill. It didn't bother the owner. He said they mostly just ate the sawdust and if they destroyed that nest, the termites would just come in from another part of the jungle.

As soon as we unloaded the wood, Nelly left for Quimistan with Pedro who rode along. Soon she was back with Doug and Juan. Of course they had letters, medicines, a newspaper, memories of fine meals in San Pedro Sula, impressions of the marketplace conditions which are unmentionable, etc., plus a large supply of *Dorados* (the better brand of local cigarettes) for themselves.

Taurino Orellana is the current *Alcalde Auxiliar*. He carries a swagger stick as the emblem of his authority. He looks physically fit with a dark complexion. He is quiet, but friendly. He came by yesterday to apologize for not helping more during our first two weeks, but he had been sick with the chicken pox. He has been watching the English and literacy classes, but hasn't participated in either. He has a reputation for being the town jokester, and for getting drunk about once a week.

Taurino returned from working in his field this afternoon and came to our house. His mood was obvious altered by the events of the day. Senor "X" had borrowed some money (for reasons he didn't share) and had arranged to pay the debt with twelve barrels of lime which the village could use to brighten up the place, including whitewashing the school. But today, Senor "X" loaded the barrels into a vehicle that took the lime out of Milparada without permission. Taurino said that this individual has nothing else of value with which to pay the debts. He is disgusted with the loss of the lime and the lack of cooperation from some members of the community. He insisted that they needed to form a group of people interested in the development of community with the power to get other

52

individuals to participate at least a little. He calmed down somewhat when we reminded him that we would be organizing a committee to run the *comedor*.

We had a more pleasant conversation with Antonio Machado and some of the other neighbors. Antonio is thirty-seven and has proven himself to be an extremely hard worker and clever improviser. He is probably the resident who is most enthusiastic about our presence. The conversation started with Juan asking what they thought we should be called. He noted that the Mexicans referred to us as *Norteamericanos* (North Americans). Antonio said, "That's not right. Canada and Mexico are also in North America. Here, you are the gringos."

"Does the name gringo have negative connotations?"

"No. The communists paint signs saying Yanqui go home, not gringo go home."

Other members of the group chimed in that the gringos are better-liked than the outsiders, including the Arab and Chinese merchants. They just come into the towns for a few days to make a fortune. "We are just Indians to them. They don't think we can do anything but labor. So, they take advantage of our poverty."

Antonio spoke up for labor. "Each man must work although he is not ordered to, that doing work is a characteristic of being man. It is one of the essential functions of the existence, along with a belief in a God." Antonio probably is not egotistical or self-righteous but he expressed an unwillingness to help a man whose need is due to his own negligence and laziness. "They can take advantage of us because we are less united."

Juan commented that it appears to him that Honduras does not have a sense of community, so they don't feel the need to aid each other. The group nodded in agreement and one of them speculated that one of reasons was the lack of organized games in which young of the same age collaborate. I was glad to hear this comment; it gives more support to the value of our recreation program for the school.

After dinner, we held our Spanish and English classes. Now we are seated around our lantern reading and writing. Soon we'll dose our bug bites and go to bed. Today we gave a pregnant woman some vitamins. Her reply when told it was free: "God will repay you." The people have the feeling of "*Que sera sera*" here. One wonders how motivation is fostered with this atmosphere of acceptance. The people seem to respond to genuine sincerity and love at any rate. We are seeing the value of our reaching out to enter their world. One example is the three month old baby that Melissa and Mary saw while they were visiting homes to speak to the women about starting health classes. The baby looked more like a three week old and was very sickly. They were able to provide some much needed powdered milk. They probably never would have seen the baby if they had waited for the mother to come to them. The rest of the team also expressed their appreciation of how much I had learned from my school visits. We know that we are getting a much deeper understanding of the country than anyone could get by being a tourist.

Thursday, July 8

This morning we began construction work on the *comedor*. Our first step was to dig a trench to extend the water line to the back of the school, where the kitchen will be. *Profesor* Jacobo questioned our route: "Why are you putting the pipe down for the *comedo*r before you are ready to use it? You should build the *comedor* first and then when it is finished you can put the pipe around it." Either he has no idea of efficiency, or he is thinking about old iron pipes that would rust. We stuck with our plan for a direct line under the future floor. With four of us working, we finished the trench in a couple of hours.

For morning recess, I started playing goalie in the soccer games. The goals are marked by a pair of rocks about seven feet apart. I'm a pretty poor soccer player, but with the narrow goal, I could pretty easily block any ball that a single kid kicked at me. When one of the boys finally passed the ball to a friend on the other side, I made only a half-hearted attempt and he scored. After that, the amount of passing and team work quickly increased. Success in scoring against me is doing much more to change their style of play than all of my previous exhortations did.

Until we get Rafael's blueprints, we are unable to actually begin work on the foundation and floor. So we decided to straighten up the area and stack the wood for the fence that we just dumped yesterday over closer to where it would be used. This activity was cut short when Doug rolled a board off of a black snake! The creature was killed with a shovel that happened to be handy at the time, after which we made a public display of this beheaded snake. School took a 15 minute break when we killed a snake outside – the teacher chatted with us about the snake and then went back in making no effort to get the kids to join her – most would have followed us as we disposed of the snake if I didn't shoo them back to school. The kids excitedly identified it as a *veneador* (venomous one).

Juan filled us in on details concerning recognition and effects of this animal. The more formal name is velvet snake. It is a relative of the cobra and its bite is usually fatal in twenty to thirty minutes, unless the victim gets a shot of the antidote before then. Considering that it would take at least that long to make the one-way trip to Quimistan, if one of us gets bit, we are effectively done for. There is one man in Quimistan who reportedly got bit on his hand while working in his field. He survived by immediately chopping off that hand with his machete. I'm sure I couldn't do that to save my life. Up to this point, I had been the only one to regularly wear combat boots. With the heat, most of the team felt more comfortable in tennis shoes or sandals. They all immediately decided to switch to boots for outdoor work.

Our activities during the afternoon: whitewashing the fences in front of the houses and the first successful completion of a CARE desk. We are mostly filling time until we get some cement.

There were no school classes this afternoon. The teachers spent the time making a crude chair from some of the rough lumber we got for the fence. A few of the kids helped. The others had an extended recess, doing whatever they felt like. We held a soccer game starting at 4:30. At 5:15 all the kids were reassembled in the school for no apparent reason and were soon dismissed from there.

Antonio came by to see Melissa as he had run a nail through his finger and apparently has not been feeling well lately.

Pedro came in after dinner and began an extremely interesting conversation over the past history of Milparada and land ownership. He claims his family has been residing here for more than a century. His grandfather told him that long ago the Spaniards had a very productive gold mine very near here. That mine accounted for the formation of Milparada. Negroes were brought in to work on the mine. According to the legend, the Viceroy visited the mine and proclaimed, "God and the angels of the sky are my slaves." After he spoke these words, the ground shook and the rocks of the mine hurled down on the people, killing most of the workers. A guard who escaped the accident ran into town yelling: "*Mala Nova*," his imperfect Spanish mispronouncing "Mala Nueva" (Bad News). So the mine area is now called "Mala no va" (Bad, don't go there). The inhabitants of Milparada believe that there are still enormous quantities of gold covered by tons of earth, and if the mine is reopened there will be a civil war as people fight over getting it all to themselves. As evidence of the existence of the gold, Pedro showed us some stones with shiny flakes. Juan and Doug quickly and quietly identified the minerals as feldspar and mice, both of which are abundant in this area.

According to some employees of the BNF (*Banco Nacional de Fomento*) all of the land in the valley was at one time owned by a single individual who sold it to an American named Harry Moser at a ridiculously low price. That was supposed to have happened eighty years ago. Moser, supposedly dead now, reportedly never bothered the squatters who live in Milparada because his primary interest was the exploitation of the timber land. Honduran law protects those who have occupied and farmed land that was not previously productive. After farming it for ten years they should be able to obtain a title. During the presidential term of Ramon Villeda Morals, Pedro Hernandez received a telegram from the President assuring him and the rest of the community of their right to occupy the land. The squatters have drawn up their own titles for parcels in the area and have been selling them. However, legally Moser or his descendants still have title to the land, and they are represented by a lawyer in San Pedro Sula. Not long ago, Pedro talked to people at the *Instituto Regional Agrario* (Regional Agrarian Institute) who told him that the proof of occupancy and other legal aspects are being revised and transactions settling boundaries will take some time. The people here are fearful of their unstable situation and have a strong guilt feeling for using land that is not legally theirs. It is almost impossible to identify who claims or holds rights to the land by virtue of occupying it.

Pedro also helped us decide which members of the community would be good candidates for the committee that would take charge of the *comedor*.

Today I heard something which reassured me that our efforts here are producing some results. As I gave the soccer ball to the small school boys, three or four of them ran off yelling "Los jugadores de Milparada" (Calling themselves the players/team of Milparada). It is a sign that residents are beginning to look upon themselves as a coordinating and cooperating group acting as a unit, instead of just a collection of separate, independent families. Our labors are starting to produce visible improvements, but the ultimate success of this project will depend on how well we can get them to develop a common bond directed toward improving their community.

Friday, July 9

Today was another calm day – with not much special going on. Pedro borrowed Antonio's oxcart and helped the boys gather river rocks that we will use for the foundation of the *comedor*. It was a dull, but necessary task.

Trinchi and Sue made three desks. Sue had trouble keeping the hand drill steady and broke both of our drill bits. Doug and I chided her, noting that the nearest drill bit was in San Pedro, so we wouldn't have a replacement until sometime next week. Sue angrily blurted out in English, "Maybe I can't drill, but I can still screw!" The local gringo watchers looked puzzled when we broke up laughing. We'll keep that one as an inside joke for the team. Antonio asked what was wrong. I showed him the broken bit and said we did not have another. He solved the problem by cutting the head off of a nail with our hack saw and carefully hammering the point flat. His bit actually worked better in the green wood than the store bought ones.

The Nurses held a meeting of the mothers of the village – only two showed up! They had planned to discuss nutrition and the *comedor* program and first aid, but since only two showed up, their plans fell through and they just discussed basic first aid. They are determined to carry out their mission, so they spent the whole afternoon they went door-to-door visiting and inviting the women to come over tomorrow at 8:30am.

Ed and Juan walked into Quimistan and confirmed that Mr. Jaquith (the Unitarian Chaplain who started the program for Cornell) is coming to see us on Monday.

For the school recess, we made full use of the CARE sports kit that the Synchronized Swimming Club of Ithaca High donated. The bag and most of the gear was clearly marked MADE IN USA. One of the kids asked what that meant. I asked the whole group, including the teachers, what they thought it stood for. *Profesor* Jacobo said, "Ma-Day in use, but I don't know what MADE is." The people here make no connection between "U.S.A." and the United States. If agencies want the goods they distribute to be associated with our country, they should mark them, "Hecho en E.E. U.U."

Among the girls, learning to jump rope is replacing volleyball as the favorite game. Every recess, several groups of girls would be jumping, learning to share and take turns turning the rope and jumping. With the long rope, the fun and success requires cooperation.

Prof. Jacobo joined me as the other goalie in playing soccer with the boys. The kids are definitely getting better at team work. Despite my best efforts on defense, my team lost two to three.

One criticism we had heard of the Cornell Project on campus is that we go down there to "play with the kids." I freely admit that I'm having fun with the kids and the recreation period is a nice break from our other labors. But there is much more to the recreation program than that. The sports are fostering a greater degree of cooperation and "team spirit." Seeing our playful side reduces the distance between us and the locals. We have clearly gained a friendly rapport with the children, which has led them to open up to us in other areas. That opens additional doors to us. Parents become friendlier when you can say nice things about their children (and when the children are presumably saying nice things about us).

Having our houses open right into the plaza also helps us get acquainted with the boys and young men, who regularly hang out there. About half of them have slingshots with them, which they use to shoot rocks at rabbits and iguanas. It is not just for sport. Any kill adds meat to their family's dinner. The older ones are back from a day in the fields, so occasionally play a little soccer, but mostly just hang out and chat.

Nicolas Cruz is fifteen years old. He told me that he just got a job as a cattle hand on a ranch on the edge of Pinalejo for thirty Lempira ($15) per month. He works three days a week. During the dry season, he had worked on a construction crew in San Pedro Sula for three months digging trenches with a pickaxe all day. With the hard labor, the pay was better, L1.50 ($0.75 a day) plus lunch. With that pay scale, he was delighted when we gave him a dime (which is the slang term for the twenty centavo coin of the same value) after he walked to Quimistan to buy some nails for us. He seems to be one of the higher status teens. He has been to Tegucigalpa. He went to school "occasionally for four years." He is one of the regulars in our literacy class. He wants to learn to read better and is proving to be a quick study. He picked up a couple of guitar chords from watching me play. He definitely likes to sing. We tried to recruit him to be part of a skit, but had to abandon the idea because he was unable to understand what drama or acting is. The idea of pretending he was someone else was totally alien to him.

His older brother Eulelio (Leo) Cruz is nineteen. He is naively curious about almost everything. Unlike his brother, he is ignorant; not just ignorant, but stupid. He doesn't talk much, other than asking questions. Tomorrow he will ask the same questions he did today and yesterday. He works on the same ranch as Nicolas, and seems to mainly follow his brother around.

My main literacy student, Juan Ramon Hernandez is fourteen. He doesn't appear to have any close friends among the other boys. The literacy class is clearly giving him a rare feeling of achievement. He now clings on to me like a hero worshipper. He is cheerful and I don't want to hurt his feelings or discourage his learning, but the fawning attachment is irritating. He is out in the fields everyday, so he hasn't participated in any of our daytime activities.

Armando DuBon is the great observer. He spent most of our first week just standing around and watching us from a distance. He is about sixteen. While he makes comments to the other teens (undoubtedly about how strange we are), he has so far avoided talking with any of us. Though yesterday when one of the younger teens started chopping some firewood for the girls, he went over with his machete and went to work with vigor.

Luis Rivera is the town playboy. He sees himself as a lady killer. He is the only teen from Milparada attending school in Pinalejo this year (and post-sixth grade at that). Luis participates in our English class and generally is one of the high status teens. He had been assigned to help up that first day when we were hauling sand. (I've found out that not all of our helpers have been volunteers. The Acalde Auxiliar drafts one or two men each work day.) He was reluctant at first and required some prodding to put his shovel to work, but once he got started, he worked hard. According to Roberto (one of the younger boys): "Luis talks about how he would help you, but he just stands around and watches. He expects you to give him whatever he wants."

We have a new player in the afternoon soccer games this week, and he is a star. Sebastiano looks very much Indian and is in his early twenties. He came to the English classes this week as well and was the best student in the class. He is better dressed than most, probably because he works for United Fruit in season. He is also very talkative and particularly enjoys chatting with the girls on the team.

Carlos Alberto Escalon wears a pin with a picture of a crucifix on it when he dresses up. I guess he is seventeen or eighteen. Yesterday he had me write down the words of a local folk song, saying that I should learn Honduran songs to sing in the United States. When I was done and showed it to him, he could not read it, but asked me to put his name on the song sheet, which I gladly did. He beamed with pride when we sang it together.

The younger boys are generally more eager to tattle on each other than to talk about themselves. Bragging definitely goes against the social grain. They are also more physically active and often give each other friendly shoves – at least most of them are friendly. This afternoon, a group of them formed a tight pack around me.

Ten-year-old Roberto DuBon is very outgoing, cheerful and energetic. He is barefoot and has tears in his shirt. His parents are the poor cousins of the richest family in town. When I asked why he wasn't in school last week, he claimed he had attended every day. The other boys snickered and told him I had been at the school for two days. His story quickly changed to, "I did miss one week because I was sick and had red bumps all over me."

Ricardo didn't want to tell me his last name. He is ten years old and doesn't go to school. "I don't like it." There are eight members in his family. He helps his big brother work their hillside field, which he says is only one *manzana* (less than two acres). He identified his big brother Juan Ramon – so much for not letting me know his last name. (In Honduras, if the parents aren't married, the child usually carries his mother's last name, so having different fathers wouldn't affect the boys' last name.) Yet he looks reasonably clean and well fed. When I first asked him, he claimed that he can read but looked embarrassed by the question. This is decidedly different than the usual proud "Yes!" that I have gotten when I asked other boys about reading. Later he admitted that he can't read and can't go to school because he has to work. He says he wants to learn to read and came to one literacy class with Juan. He enjoyed liked it and learned two pages in the *Alfalit* book that day. When he left, he told me that he would come back every day, but he hasn't returned. When I asked him about it today, Ricardo replied, "My parents don't want me to be outside of the house after dark."

Juan Borjas Orbina stopped by briefly. He is a cute and active eight year old in the first grade class. He is a poor student who can't read yet, not even recognizing the first letters of the alphabet. He enjoys rough housing during the recesses. He was carting a bucket of water he had just filled from our backyard tap. When I reached out and suggested that he come over and join the group, he took off like a scared rabbit. "What's he afraid of? Did I do something to scare him?"

Roberto replied, "He's not afraid of you. He's afraid of his parents. They will beat him with a stick if he takes too long getting water." The other boys nodded in solemn agreement.

Geronimo Hernandez is the namesake son of the man who owns the girls' house. He lives with his mother and two sisters. (His father has another "wife" living with him in the house near Quimistan. When I asked him about school, he said he doesn't go any more because he graduated last year with distinction. He said he spent four years in school because the first year was lost. They had a teacher who was always tardy and didn't teach anything. (That matches what Jacobo had told me about the prior teachers.) He wears shoes and his shirt is clean and intact. He says that he works in the field occasionally. Mostly I see him hanging around town, especially outside the store. He usually shows up at the school at recess time to join the soccer games with the younger kids. He often volunteers to help our team with construction task. Today he commented on how strong I was for a skinny person. He was particularly impressed by having seen me carrying a full sack on cement on my shoulder. I told him, "That does not require a lot of muscle if you lift it right. The secret is to keep you back straight, bend your knees and quickly swing the bag while you stand up. Do you want me to show you how?"

"Yes."

"Can I use you to be the cement bag?" That brought giggles and then an okay. So I bent down, grabbed him by the waist and swung him up on my shoulder. It thrilled him and the others. Roberto immediate wanted a turn, followed by a couple of others. Then they asked me to "Do it to Juancito."

Juancito Marin is one of the tallest first graders, but he is also very skinny except for a bulging stomach. The first time that I saw him he had an obvious chicken pox rash, but he was carrying a full bucket of water to a small hut. He set the bucket down by the door and starting chopping firewood. I wondered why he wasn't lying in bed. He was fully recovered by the time I visited the school. Juancito stood out as being extremely jumpy and fidgety. During recess, he runs up and down the field, but avoids contact with the other boys.

When I flipped him up to my shoulder, he almost slipped out of my hands and over my back. He is amazingly light – no more than twenty-five or thirty pounds. When his stomach hit my shoulder, he groaned. I quickly lifted him up to above my head and gently lowered him to the ground. Just as quickly, his smile returned. It is scary to think of the future of a seven year old who is so light. The tapeworm in his stomach must be getting more nourishment out of his food than he does.

Marcos Hernandez looks like he's eleven, so I guessed his age as twelve. Oops, he's actually fourteen years old. He keeps clean; his clothes are in good condition, though the material for his shirt obviously came from a flour sack. He is quiet and submissive when his father is present, but very talkative when the adults aren't around. He tells me he started school when he was seven and finished in three years. Since then, he has worked in the field everyday, weeding corn and gathering firewood. Their family *milpa* is in the hills, about a fifteen minute walk from his house. Marcos reads syllable by syllable, rather slowly in a sweet voice, but he clearly knows the meaning of what he has just read. He started our first conversation by asking what the English words are for different things. He is fascinated by my English-Spanish dictionary, and is able to sound out the printed English words. After only a brief explanation, he is able to use it to look up words for himself. He is also fascinated by our steel tape measure. He adds and subtracts well, mostly in his head. He multiplies with difficulty. He comes to the English classes and loves the *Loteria* games. By the end of our first week, he has learned to read my numberless watch and tell time.

In answer to one of my questions, Marcos told me that he has no idea of why we came here. He asked how much it costs to fly to the United States, because he wants to go there someday. He has never actually seen an airplane. The farthest away he has ever been is San Marcos (twenty kilometers up the road). "It is bigger than Milparada, but it is ugly and full of flies. Quimistan is pretty." He is firm about being a Catholic, even though he doesn't go to church. He equates Protestants with the Evangelical Mission in Pinalejo. Marcos adamantly says he is a Liberal, but also says there is very little difference between them and the Nationalists. He didn't recognize the name General Lopez as president, but knew the president is a Nationalist and assumes he is a good man. He readily told me, "There are no communists in Honduras, only in Cuba. Fidel Castro is a bad man. The Cubans fight." But he wouldn't give me an opinion of people from the United States. He doesn't know what CARE or the Peace Corps is, but identifies the Alliance for Progress as the clinic. He has seen a doctor twice in his life.

A couple of times Marcos has quietly asked me for food, but doesn't beg from any of the others. After dinner this evening, he hungrily asked for a piece of bread. I slipped him the left over end of our dinner loaf – which he then shared with Roberto, and saved a little piece for his sister. His older brother isn't home most of the time; he is off working in a lumber camp. He has five big sisters, four of whom are married, one little brother and two little sisters. He is contented with his current life in Milparada.

The meals today were very good. It's really great what a difference fruits and vegetables make in the diet. Tonight's literacy class and English class were good. The week has been very calm – probably the calm before the storm!

Saturday, July 10

We've gone about as far as we can go without the plans for the *comedor* construction. So we puttered the day away.

This morning Trinchi, Sue, Doug and Ed took a Jeep ride with Rolando and Guillermo of *Banco de Fomento* to a small, pretty, town in the mountains. Juan and I laid the pipe for the *comedor's* water tap. It was a short job. We were done before the school's recess. Then Juan set out to make an informal survey of the town while *Profesor* Jacobo and I played soccer with the boys. On request of the kids (who weren't allowed in the evening sessions) I conducted an English class for the third graders. Their attention was a little better than during their regular classes. We basically covered "Hello", "Good morning", "Good afternoon", "Good night", "Please", "Thank you" and counting to ten. It was entirely oral – I wasn't ready to attempt to explain such English spelling as the silent "gh" in night. *Profesora* Maria Luis was more of a nuisance than a help.

Nobody showed up for their health class, so Melissa and Mary washed clothes and ran their normal clinic. They are mighty discouraged about the lack of participation in their classes, but are determined to keep trying.

Trinchi and I walked to Quimistan for a little shopping and a chat with the *Amigos de Honduras*. The volunteer doctor said he sees 100 patients a day - ("disgusting"). He believes that a lot of his infant patients will die from lack of food, especially milk. When we told him about the free powdered milk available from CARE, he shrugged and said, "That's not part of my project." He disapproved of our project: "You should be using your heads, not your hands . . . You should pay the peasants fifty cents a day for doing that stuff." (At least he knew the standard wage for laborers). I'm realizing that there is a giant difference in attitude between doing something for others and doing something with them.

The teen volunteers were mostly unhappy and bored. "There's nothing to do around here. We can't even watch television." And "Nobody speaks English." They are bunking on cots in the Alliance clinic, an austere setting. They have a food allowance of three dollars a day (which is ample) and don't do any of their own cooking. They didn't go through a screening program and had only a few hours of training. Their main qualifications are the ability to pay for the trip plus a charitable desire to do good. They are undoubtedly doing good by giving vaccinations, but they will be returning home with bitter memories and no understanding of the country or their clients. While I dislike the doctor, I just feel sorry for these kids.

We heard some resentment from townspeople in Quimistan about their lack of getting around town; "They keep to gringos for company." But, they still have a good reputation because "They care."

Some of the Rotarians have expressed harsher judgments:

"Most have no knowledge of our country."

"Tourists!"

"The doctors are just out for publicity."

"There are three types: religious moralists, boy scouts (most of the kids), and then there are those others. Only about one in twenty is really bad."

Trinchi and I had cooking detail today, and got adventurous. We tried to make and *plantano* fritters, which turned out more like pancakes with lumps of bananas in them. Dinner was more successful. We made pizza, from unleavened dough, tomato paste and mixed vegetables with a little goat cheese (the only kind that was available in the Quimistan store). It was not your standard pizza, but it still tasted good. Like every other dinner, we also cooked up a batch of rice in the pressure cooker. I have to admit the pressure cooker makes that job quick and easy. The after meal clean up has become just another routine.

While we were eating, Don Pedro and Jacobo started a volleyball game with ten teenagers and young men. That continued until it was too dark to see the ball. Then we went into the schoolhouse for entertainment. Instead of a dance, this week we had a guitar and song session conducted mostly by the townspeople. The three people who had told me that they played the guitar showed their stuff, passing my guitar around.

There is a slight build up of strain in the group. The novelty has worn off. Our chores have become just tedious chores. We have too much time on our hands and are stymied by the lack of materials for our main project. I expect our moods will improve and the team spirit will return when the material for the *comedor* gets here.

Sunday, July 11

Sunday is a day of rest – and that is what today was. Today began with a much appreciated precedent (I hope it is a precedent) of waking up at 6:00 instead of 5:30.

Trinchi had a very interesting talk with a woman from Milparada whom we had never met before. She said that the other women had told her not to bother coming to the classes because our women couldn't understand anything they said. Another discouragement for our nurses; they had thought they had been getting the major points across. She is from a southern province originally and had some criticisms of the Milparada people. She remarked that they are lazy and do not take advantage of the opportunities that they do have. Their poverty is at least partially self-imposed. We have had similar feelings at times. Antonio Machado and Eduardo DuBon, the carpenter, work hard and quietly. The majority of the others spend a lot of time standing around. Pedro is sometimes included in this group and he is beginning to bug us a little. He is more talk than action, although of course he is earnest, and manages to successfully interrupt our work by puttering around. Trinchi and Susan spent half a day yesterday redoing a desk he made. Things like that make it hard to remember to appreciate good intentions. We have enough frustration coming from the inefficiency of our own labor with the limited tools at hand. Our most frequent use of English has become muttered cussing.

Rafael drove up with the sketched plans for the *comedor* (complete with dimensions). He advised that we make a rock filled foundation two feet deep and another foot above the ground so it will be strong enough if they ever add brick walls.

He did better than keep his word from last week. He brought us pineapples and hamburgers – real meat for lunch! He is always a very welcome guest. Tomorrow we can start the real construction work. It doesn't look too hard. The floor will be a slab twenty-six feet long and eighteen feet wide. The main supports will be four concrete pillars ten feet eight inches tall, to match the school walls. We can use some of the two-inch pipes that are lying around in the place of rebar. We will need to build four A-frame trusses to support the roof. Two will be over the pillars; the other two will be supported by 4"x4" pieces of lumber. We should be able to complete it in less than three weeks.

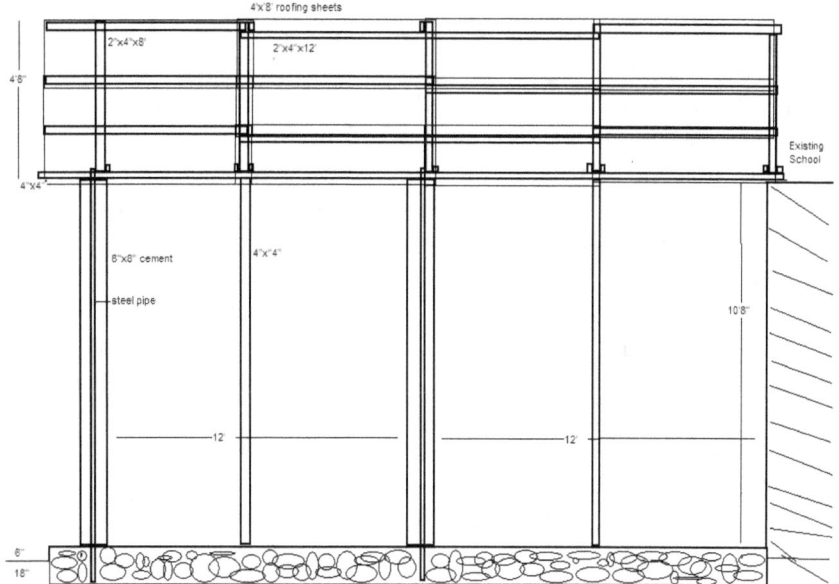

Figure 3. Comedor plan - side view

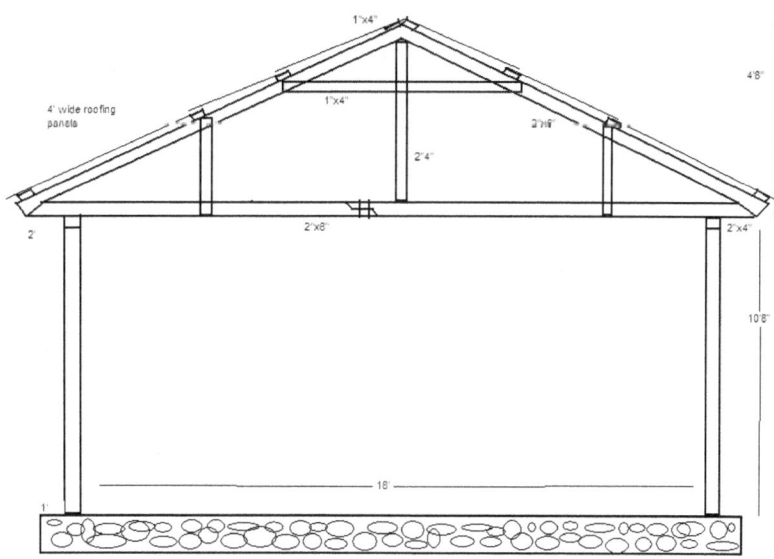

Figure 4. Comedor plan - end view

67

Marcos invited me to see his *milpa*, insisting that it be just the two of us. He chatters away as we hike, carrying our machetes. He likes to play with Bartito and the school kids more than with the older teens. Eight people live in his house, but his older brother is away working in a lumber camp; it is a good job. He has some baby dogs. "Are there dogs in the United States?" (Yes) "Do you have a dog?" (Not now, but my parents do.)

He eagerly told me about all the different plants around. We stopped at one tree for him to cut open a big berry with a hard white rind and show me the juice. This sap was the same color and consistency of Elmer's glue. He called it, "*leche de fruta de Mico*" and said that it was good for rubbing on sore backs from working. The parrots eat this fruit. "There are many rabbits, parrots, lizards and mosquitoes in the hills." I saw one parrot, two small lizards and more than enough mosquitoes. We also saw non-biting wood ants carrying leaves along a fallen trunk.

When we reached the *milpa*, I was surprised at how steep the slope was. It must about a forty-five degree angle. Marcos, his father and younger cousin Bartito ploughed with a machete, hacking holes for the seeds. The rocks and stumps from last years "slash and burn" clearing are still in place. They have cantaloupes and beans growing between corn plants. The total field is two *manzanas* (three and a half acres). It is partly choked with weeds. Marcos and Bartito do the weeding by machete. "You have to be careful not to cut any of the melon vines or bean plants." He said some other farmers use a hoe or wood plough for weeding. "They don't hurt your back so much, but they aren't good on the steep hills." When weeding, they just leave the cut weeds lying on the field. They grow back quickly, so you have to cut them again. If they made a bigger field, there would be too many weeds to keep out.

There are several avocado trees and one lime tree on one edge of the field. A stream runs along this edge. Marcos pointed out a small broad-leafed water plant that he says is good to eat, but we didn't try it today.

The overgrown land on the other side is their old field. In about four more years they will the current field won't be good for growing, so they'll burn and clear the next section. The stream includes his bathing place. His father rigged a 3 foot long hollow cane to make a "shower" over a six-inch deep pool. It is a cool shaded oasis. He normally eats lunch here. The workers carry three tortillas and a gourd full of water to the fields to take care of their mid-day break.

Before returning, we chopped some kindling and each of us carried a bundle back to his house for firewood.

While we were gone, the school boys went to Pinalejo for a soccer game against the Pinalejo school's second and third grade students. They came back elated. They had won six to two. One of them told me that this was the first time they beat Pinalejo. "We scored so much because we kicked the ball to each other." I am filled with more pride than I deserve.

At dinner we had a good talk about religion which everyone enjoyed. It started because of Melissa's Bible reading. Melissa is a devout Southern Baptist. The rest of us range from lapsed Catholic through liberal protestant to downright cynical agnostic. So the discussion was lopsided in favor of doubts about churches and the Biblical accuracy. Melissa is a good sport and did a good job of defending her staunch position.

Monday, July 12

We woke up to a surprise. A scorpion had fallen off the rafter and landed in Juan's open suitcase. Because of the mothballs he packed, the scorpion was dead. It was pure luck that it didn't land on one of us in our sleep. The suitcases were on our spare, "guest" cot, so if he had waited one more day, the scorpion would have landed on Jaquith's head instead of the mothballs. We are going to be extra careful about shaking out our boots in the morning before putting them on.

I just finished writing a letter home:

Hello everybody,

I got Dad's letter (postmarked June 29) and Carol's thank you note and enjoyed them both.

The daily schedule is rather tiring. Up at 5:30. Breakfast at 6:30, work at 7:00. A half-hour break at 9:15 for me to run the school's recreation program for the boys, mostly soccer. Back to work 'til noon, lunch, siesta (which I usually spend talking to the kids, back to work by 2:00. Recreation again 3:00 to 3:30 (give or take 30 minutes). Supper at 6:00. At 7:00, literacy and English classes in the school three days a week. (I'm working on English which is in amazingly high demand - mostly a status symbol, I think.) The other nights, there is bingo.

About 9:00, all the town goes to bed and we put on swim suits for a shower (not enclosed) and write up our notes and talk things over.

Today we began excavation for the Comedor foundation. Although we constantly participated in the physical labor, the major part of this work was done by the town's people. Two men were selected daily by the auxiliary mayor to work as our assistants, and fortunately this policy was kept up the entire summer. For some reason or another, our work inevitably attracted attention, so that it was not unusual to have at least five or six men helping by the end of the day. Some of those men would work day or night if the need arose.

Love,   Dick

The guys spent the day digging the foundation while our helpers gathered more rocks for filling our trench.

Sue has proved to be an able carpenter and Trinchi a worthy first mate for assembling desks. Neither drives a very straight nail. That's not an issue. Here bent nails, however old, are straightened out by hammering and re-used. They are adamant about doing some "men's work" to set an example of equality.

At almost 4:30 Don Lelo arrived in a cloud of dust in the jeep piloted by the amiable Rolando of the Banco Nacional de Fomento and Paul Jaquith from Cornell. We are always happy to see an old friend visit. They joined our dinner. Rolando left right after dinner. Lelo walked around talking with townsfolk. Jaquith went to bed early.

The literacy and English classes occupied the accustomed 6:30 pm slot on the schedule. One boy, Nicolas Cruz, asked to borrow books from our CARE library – shortly followed by some of his friends. I was quite pleased that some of the teens had a desire to read.

Tuesday, July 13

Today Pedro Hernandez, Don Lelo, Jaquith, Charlie Garcia and Guillermo Rivera were with us all day. Well, Jaquith was only kind of with us. He was still tired and not feeling well. He did almost nothing but sleep.

The two from the Alliance for Progress Mobile Health Unit came prepared to initiate a latrine project by making a pair for the school. They supplied the forms, etc. for the cement stools, and left them with us so we could help the villagers make more for their homes.

Charlie noted that *Alianza Para el Progreso* has two linguistically correct translations. While it is supposed to be "for progress", the opponents translate it as "The Alliance stops the progress." The second usage became popular when an Alliance funded highway improvement project got bogged down in politics, leaving a half-built bridge conspicuously going nowhere from the edge of San Pedro.

Charlie and Doug built cement bases for the school's new latrines. Charlie wrote "Cornell Student 1965" with a stick in the wet cement.

Pedro and the rest of the gang finished filling the foundation trench with rocks and we started pouring cement to hold them firmly in place. We have built a wooden trough with a sheet of plywood as the bottom for mixing concrete, so now we can mix a full bag at a time with sand and water, using shovels to get a proper consistency. It is much more efficient than the laundry tub we used for our house floors.

In the afternoon we had a very successful meeting with members of the community. As the people were gathering, I noticed the school's next door neighbor stayed at home and was peering over his fence. This Senor Cruz is a very low status man. He wears cheap sandals, not shoes, and very ragged clothes. He keeps a pig in his yard. He lives with his son, one of the third graders, and seldom mixes with other townspeople. He has a small field in the hills but he is often hanging around his home during the work day. He is also the town barber, giving a haircut and a shave for L0.50 (one quarter). Senor Cruz came into the school during one of the literacy lessons. He acted surprised when I spoke to him and offered him a pencil and paper. He said he wanted nothing and left a few minutes later.

We held the meeting in front of the school. The turnout was too great for everyone to fit inside. We had over a hundred people, including a few new faces. I never was introduced to the town elder, a gentleman with a white beard who uses a walking stick and moves slowly. Marcos told me that he is seventy years old and still works in his field all day. He stood and listened to the proceedings with a quiet dignity. Leonidas Pinto, one of last night's guitar players, came back for the meeting. He looks pure Caucasian Spanish and is relatively well off. He lives on a *hacienda* about two miles beyond the town, but he still volunteered to serve on the committee.

Guillermo explained the benefits of the *comedor* and how it would help with their children's nutrition and illness problems. Don Lelo gave his already famous talk on "*Unidos Todos, Americanos Todos, de Pole a Pole*". Juan explained the requirements for organizing and operating the program. He stressed the need for a democratic, cooperative committee to run it, if it were to be a success. Jaquith snapped the usual amount of pictures. Eight members of the community volunteered for the *Comite del Comedor Infantile*. Afterward a number of folks said they were all happy with the very democratic procedure for the initial meeting. We hadn't taken any votes, so I guess in their minds any meeting that is not dominated by a single authority giving instructions is "democratic." We will hold another meeting in a couple of weeks for the final selection of the committee and the members' duties.

After the meeting we discovered Guillermo's musical ability. We all sat around him and listened to some very good guitar playing (far superior to mine).

Wednesday, July 14

Today is Bastille Day, a school holiday.

It is my turn to run errands in San Pedro. I took Marcos Hernandez with me. It is the first time he has seen a real city. It has been a great experience for both of us. I got up early; Marcos was already waiting outside. We walked to Pinalejo with Lelo and Jaquith to catch the 6:00 bus. As soon as we got off the bus, we went our separate ways.

The day's business went very well – much more smoothly than my last visit to San Pedro. I made arrangements with CARE for wood for twenty-five desks to be delivered to Chiquila (a village in the Quimistan district that is a candidate for a team next year). I also met with the U.S.I.S (United States Information Service) to have their mobile film unit to make a visit to show movies in Milparada. They are scheduled to come on Saturday, August 7. It falls at the same time that our team will off visiting Copan, so we'll miss it, but it will still be a treat for the village. I also completed the usual shopping chores. I bought some varnish and more tools at Larach's hardware store. *Don* Jacobo Larach treated Marcos and me to lunch then sent pencils to all the school kids. We ran into Don Lelo four times and each time heard the same admonition: "Most important, Tell Juan to be sure and lock the latrine." I have no idea of why we would do that.

Marcos was wide-eyed and quiet all day, but said he likes the place. He was much more timid than normal. When other people were around, he stayed close behind me, despite my encouragement to come forward. There were so many things that were new to him.

We grabbed breakfast when we first arrived. I ordered fried eggs with toast and milk for each of us. It was obvious that he wasn't used to eating with a fork. I had to show him how to use its side to cut his eggs. The cold milk brought a happy smile. Everything he had ever eaten was either tepid or hot off the stove. This afternoon I bought him an ice cream cone. The first lick brought a startled response followed by another big smile. That led to a discussion about snow. He had seen pictures of white topped mountains, but had no idea of what snow was.

Marcos was hopelessly confused by traffic. He stopped at the first smooth painted wall, stroked it and smiled, "Beautiful, very gentle." He didn't particularly like the hamburger at lunch. The electric fan in the café was much more fascinating. Other novelties included electric light bulbs, pavement, a railroad track and train, a fire truck with its siren running and climbing the stairs to the top of the municipal building. The biggest thrill was the supermarket. (I went to get some spices and real cheese.) He was totally in awe, "So much food, so many kinds!"

We got back to the marketplace only to find out that the 4:00 bus had gotten a good load and left an hour early. Marcos looked panicky. I explained that this wasn't a problem. We could stay at the Swanson's house. We would get a good dinner and a good bath. Marcos insisted that he had to go back today because he has to work tomorrow. So I lugged my flour sack (with two gallons of varnish, some tools and some lighter items) across town to the "highway," trying to hitch a ride along the way. It was my turn to start feeling panic. I envisioned walking along the road all night, stranded in the middle of nowhere.

On the edge of town, we encountered a truck with two men stopped at the brickyard. They were headed to Santa Gertrudis, on the other side of Quimistan. They agreed to give us a ride if we helped load the truck with bricks. The bricks were lying in a loose pile on the ground. It took about forty-five minutes to stack them neatly in the back of the truck. The driver and assistant filled the cab, leaving Marcos and I to stand on the bricks in the back. The rain started late today, as we approached Cofradia. We were soon uncomfortably soaked. The driver kindly pulled into a gas station (he said it was for my sake) to wait out the main storm. He was quite curious about why a Gringo was hitchhiking. He thought we all were rich and had cars. I explained that I was a student with very little money, at least until I finished school. We got dropped off in Quimistan after dark, and luckily ran into Rolando, who offered us a ride to Milparada.

Marcos remained wide-eyed from the time we got on the bus until we returned to Quimistan. I asked him, "Would you like to live in San Pedro?"

"No, I want you to take me to the United States with you."

While we were gone, the rest of the team had a busy morning - boys working on the *comedor* foundation; girls making desks, washing, cooking and recreating with the school children. The afternoon was a slow. The water supply was cut off somewhere up the line, so the men couldn't make cement. It was hot day with no breeze, so the women decided not to work either. Mary and Melissa went on goodwill visits around town visiting with the women and giving health advice. The rest of the team went on a goodwill visit for their stomachs to Pinalejo and bought sweet fruit treats – which turned out to be bad will for their stomachs. They got caught by the afternoon rain on the walk home. The team had an early dinner, then waited for the literacy classes to start, but the rain continued, so only a few students showed up. So while Susan and Trinchi taught, Ed examined and sorted the scorpions he had collected earlier in the day.

That's when I arrived back in Rolando's jeep (along with Carlos and the mayor of Quimistan). Carlos borrowed my guitar and entertained us with songs, throwing in jibes and insults aimed at the mayor. Not to be outdone, I sang "*Coplas*" – a Mexican song full of sexual double-entendres.

As the hour gets later, our itching gets fiercer. When our visitors left we could scratch and paint ourselves with calamine lotion in peace. I wonder if the natives develop some degree of immunity, or are just used to feeling itchy all the time. Melissa has defined our medical condition (multiple layers of bug bites and rashes) as the "Creeping Chinese Rot," predicting no real relief.

We are learning more about this town, these people and their habits. Perhaps it is good that we are going to the crowded capital city of Tegucigalpa to be able to appreciate our quiet, peaceful and unpretentious little hamlet. Our projects are really underway now and everybody keeps very busy. The villagers continue to come each day to help. This is the most encouraging sign.

Friday, July 15

We're talking about on how the time has flown. This weekend will mark the half-way point in our stay. Tonight will truly fly by since we'll be rising at 3:30am to begin our trip to Tegulcigalpa. Today began as usual except for an exploding kerosene stove. Somehow the flame got down into the reservoir and BAM. Nobody got hurt and nothing else caught fire. We still have three that work, plus our wood stove.

No work on the *comedor* today. The desk building and varnishing continues. We need to let the base cement cure before adding the smooth top layer. We found a second velvet snake in the wood pile by the school; at least it was smaller. We all wonder where its six-foot mother may be.

The school children have been working vigorously on a vegetable garden behind the school building. They have completed fencing it in (to keep out animals) and are now breaking up the soil with hoes and pickaxes. Today, one little boy stepped on a nail and Melissa gave him a tetanus injection. He grimaced but didn't let out a sound.

I've been monitoring the progress on a house under construction at the edge of the village. I walk by it every couple of days to see how the work is progressing. Two young men are doing the construction; neither is the owner. It will be occupied by a pair of newlyweds who aren't in town now. Most of the time, they have finished for the day before I get my afternoon stroll, so I have been able to examine it without seeming too nosy.

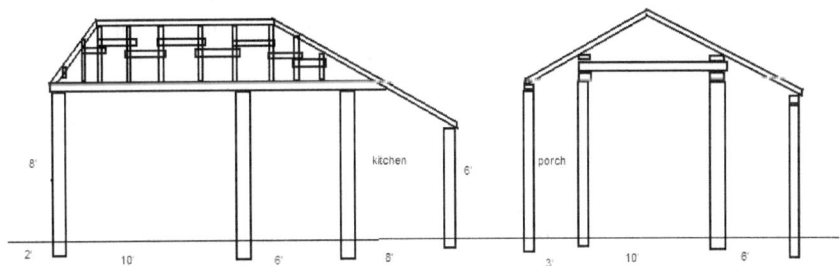

Figure 5. House building

The main supports, both vertical posts and top cross beams are more or less ten-inch diameter logs hewn from larger trunks. The posts are ten feet long with the bottom two feet buried in the ground. (They aren't set in concrete.) The secondary supports and ridgepoles are six inches square. The rest of the wood is a combination of thin lathes of varying width and small round branches. They first built the frame and put on a tile roof that extends about a foot beyond the outside wall. The tiles are laid directly on the lathes, with no tarpaper or other sealant. After the roof was complete, they filled in the frame, except for the two framed doorways, using vertical slats (nailed at top to the cross beam) and small branches interwoven horizontally. A "foundation" of rocks and mud about eight inches tall was built around the base, securing the bottom of the slats. To finish the walls, one man worked from the inside while the other was working from the outside. Both of them hand pressed mud (with a little straw or dead grass mixed in) into the frame. They left the twigs free of mud where the windows will go. The floor plan is a single large room, like the girls' house. While the mud was drying, they built the stove at one end. The stove is a three-foot by three-foot adobe platform, two feet tall. Then they molded a mud U-shaped ridge (with an air vent in back) sized to support the top of an oil drum about eight inches above the platform. After the mud had dried, they went back and cut out the windows. The windows were finished by fitting a wooden frame into the wall and fastening wooden shutter by hinges on top of the frame. The windows are propped open with a stick against the bottom sill. The doors in town are universally Dutch doors, so the tops can be left open for ventilation without animals coming in. None of the wood was sealed or painted. The total construction time with two workers was about three weeks. The men tell me that the smaller stick and thatch houses could be built in five days.

This afternoon, the boys walked to Quimistan to get the mail (and have a beer). The young ladies in the post office asked Doug and Ed to marry them. There is no question that Doug is the best looking catch. They are both physically attractive. They told us they are good cooks and would do all of our laundry and cleaning as well. When Doug and Ed said, "No thank you," they made me the same offer. From their vantage point, all gringos are rich and marriage to any gringo would be their passport to the United States. It is hard to think of myself as rich, but compared to the standard of living here, even an impoverished student in the United States is living a life of luxury.

I talked to Roberto's dad, Senor Escalon, this afternoon. He is twenty-seven to thirty years old, and barefooted. His first contact with team was coming to Melissa with a sore toe; he is proud of the bandage she put on his foot. He assured me that everyone in Milparada is our friend. He thought we were leaving for good. When I told him we'd be back, he answered, "To where? Which town?" I couldn't convince him that we would return to Milparada.

This evening all of Pedro's family came over for a chat and to wish us well on our journey. They wanted us to know that our stuff will be safe. Antonio will be sleeping in the boys' house; Pedro in the girls' and the Auxiliary Mayor will patrol the houses during the daytime to make sure our stuff is not bothered. Until they brought it up, I hadn't considered the possibility that anyone would steal any of our possessions.

Friday, July 16

This is the real Friday. I got ahead of myself with yesterday's entry. It is hard to keep the days straight around here. However, today's experiences will stand out in our memories. Our sleep was interrupted by a VW bus horn at approximately 3:15 am, fifteen minutes ahead of our alarm. We left for San Pedro about 3:50 am. The driver headed off through the dark using only parking lights. His headlights had burned out some time ago. We arrived in San Pedro by 6:00 am, allowing our driver time to make his normal morning route, just a couple of hours late. We met a well-rested Jaquith in the Columbia Hotel and enjoyed a hearty breakfast. The bus for Tegucigalpa was scheduled to pick us up about 8:00.

Our bus actually left at 9:15 am with forty-seven passengers crammed into an old school bus designed for thirty-six children. An upright piano was loaded in back, blocking the emergency exit. Buses are usually almost full to way overcrowded; we passed one with three passengers on the top luggage rack. For some unknown reason, it was necessary to make four stops for gas, oil, passengers, and God knows what else before we reached La Lima, fifteen kilometers away. La Lima is at the junction of the road to El Progreso. A fellow passenger informed me that "El Progreso is the garbage can of Honduras. It is the home of many thieves and professional gun men." He explained that it is a dangerous place because there is no capital punishment in Honduras. It was abolished to end the political exterminations that followed early government coups. So murderers are often released after a couple of years.

At any rate, we did not begin a sustained drive until we left La Lima about 10:15. The next ten-and-a-half hours were extremely interesting but tiring for all. Tegulicgalpa is about 175 kilometers from San Pedro Sula as the crow flies, but more than twice as far as the road winds. We saw a real cross-section of the country.

Before lunch we drove along the shore of *Lago de Yojoa*. It is the biggest lake in Honduras and provides the country's only hydroelectric dam at the outlet. It is mediocre in size, much smaller than the dams I'm used to seeing in Arizona. The modern hydroelectric plant serves the Tegucigalpa area and all of the North Coast (except La Ceiba) while operating at only a fraction of its capacity. La Ceiba has a small oil burning plant on the coast. Most of the other towns that have electricity rely on diesel generators.

We stopped for lunch in Taulabe at 12:45 pm. The meal was served on a covered patio. The place doesn't look clean, so we order conservatively. I had a big bowl of beans with tortillas. We got under way again at 1:30pm. The next section of road was particularly rocky and rutted. This is a downhill stretch. The uphill vehicle has the right of way, so every time we met another vehicle, we were required to pull to the side, stop and turn out lights. We didn't reach Siguatepeque, twenty-six kilometers away until 2:50 pm. Siguatepeque is the geographic center of the country. It is a relatively nice town - most of the houses are painted and have flowers planted in front.

From here on, the road again narrows and twists along the mountain side. We're going up hill, so we have the right of way. The slopes are steeper now, too steep for agriculture. Wherever there is a relatively level area, we pass a small settlement with patches of corn. I didn't see any mud houses, just small homes constructed of sticks. The Indian blood is thicker in the central plateau, nearly all of the people have a dark complexion. At the river crossings, the women doing their laundry are bare to the waist. Many of the boys (up to about twelve to fourteen years old) are running around the clearings completely nude. I spotted a woman whipping a little kid with a horsewhip. At one turn in the road, I glimpsed a particularly dramatic tableau. A horse was rearing up on his hind legs in a small clearing with a single house. It had a rope around its neck with a boy tugging on the other end. The picture would have made the cover of the National Geographic, but before I could have dug out my camera, we had gone around two more curves.

At 4:45 pm, we pulled into the old colonial capital of Comayagua. It has the oldest church in the country. The church is similar in style to the old Spanish missions in Arizona. Unlike San Xavier De Bac, this historic church is very run down. We are entering the mining district. The soil is gets worse and we see less agriculture as we near Tegulcigalpa. The grazing livestock were wearing forked-stick collars so they don't get their heads stuck between the strands of barbed wire in the fences.

We got a half-hour dinner stop at 7:00 pm in the shabby little town of La Lima.

It is getting dark as we approach Comaguela, Tegucigalpa's twin city. We pass through the red light district which features about fifty whore houses on the main street into Tegucigalpa. The street was empty except for a few women leaning against doorways and smoking.

We bounced (literally) into Tegucigalpa about 9:00 pm, thus terminating a nineteen hour trip. Although it was decidedly an extremely worthwhile trip, the team decided to look into returning by airplane.

We're staying at Dona Teresa's *pension* (hostel). It is across the street from the *Cuerpo Especial de Seguridad*. The *pension* is a rambling structure – several large rooms with six beds per room and two bathrooms. The room rate which includes three meals (our first one was plain but good) is six *lempira* (the dollars) per day. We joined the other Cornell-Honduras team here. They are stationed in Lepaterigue, a town about forty kilometers from here.

Saturday, July 17

Tegulcigalpa is at an altitude of about 3800 feet with a population of 150,000 (not counting the suburbs). In general the architecture is ghastly, much worse construction than San Pedro. As we walk around we encountered relatively few shoeshine boys (or boys hanging out looking for errands), but the ones that we see appear relatively well off. In contrast to San Pedro most of the shoe shine boys have manufactured white shirts and shoes of their own.

Well, we missed the President. We were told that is he was sick and unable to see us. The newspaper mentioned his presence at a reception yesterday, so I suspect that the reported illness is just an excuse and that he just isn't interested in meeting a group of students. We did not let that disappointing start spoil our day – it became, instead, the Ambassabor's Day.

After not seeing the President, we all went to the American Embassy. It is by far the fanciest, most modern building in town. It looks like a brick fortress, surrounded by a tall wall, so that from the sidewalk about all you can see is the American flag flying from an even taller pole. Although in my mind I questioned the image that is projected by such an ostentatious show of power, I still felt a surge of pride at seeing the Stars and Stripes waving over us. We met the new American Ambassador, Mr. J.J. Jova (all of nine days on the job) and his Consulate, Mr. Fisher. Ambassador Jova is still getting organized. He is simple and straightforward talker. He complained about the food at the official residence being too fancy and complimented our projects, especially since we were getting out into the rural areas where most of the population lives. Mr. Fisher is a career Foreign Service officer who has been stationed in Honduras for years.

We talked for about an hour in his private office – about the political and economic plight of Honduras. Since Mr. Jova is such a newcomer, Mr. Fisher did most of the talking – we learned a lot and enjoyed the conversation immensely.

The President, General Lopez is not an intellectual; he has only a seventh grade education. He is well-intentioned, and knows he is no politician. He leaves politics up to his aides (or cohorts) who are apparently not very good. Currently all local officials are appointed by the central government. Some of them are more interested in feathering their own nests rather than improving the country. General Lopez puts great stress on the maintenance of law and order.

One sign of progress is the increased presence of automobiles. In 1950, there were only 3,000 motor vehicles in the entire country; a thousand of those were owned by United Fruit. Now there are over 17,000 (many of them new). The most common are VW's of all types, Jeeps, Mercedes Benz trucks, then Tokoyta (a Japanese imitation of Jeep) and secondhand U.S. trucks and school buses. Passenger cars made in the United States are scarce, partly because they are not designed for the conditions of the Honduran roads and partly because of price. The import duties on new cars make them cost double what they are in the United Sates, so there is little difference in cost between a Ford and a Mercedes. Incidentally, the local joke is that FORD stands for *Fabricada Ordinaria, Reparaciones Diarias* (assembled indifferently, needing repairs daily).

Honduran society has almost a caste system based on race. Pure-blood Spaniards and other Europeans are at the top. *Mestizos* are the next layer and Indians are generally considered to be inherently and intellectually inferior. (The Chinese community, mostly merchants and store keepers, keeps to itself and is not integrated into the general society.) Mr. Fisher told us of one bright young man who was born in an Indian village on the Mosquito Coast. When he got his driver's license, the official looked at his birth certificate and said there was a mistake; no Indian could pass the driver's test. So he issued the man a driver's license that identified him as a *Mestizo*. The man was a successful entrepreneur. He bought a used truck and eventually built up a fleet. He recently incorporated his trucking firm. The articles of incorporation identify him as Spanish. Thus the official documents help confirm the racial stereotypes.

We also got the story behind Chiquita bananas. A few years ago, a fungus started attacking the banana plantations all over Central America. United Fruit was unable to concoct a way to kill it without destroying the trees so they concentrated on finding a variety of bananas that was resistant to the fungus. Plantains are apparently immune, but they aren't sweet enough for the export market. After hundreds of tries, they did develop a good sweet tasting variety, but it had two drawbacks. It was smaller and the peel is thinner and bruises easily. The bunches couldn't be simply stacked in the holds of ships like the old standard, they had to be separated into smaller clumps and packed in boxes before shipping. Both of these drawbacks were countered by a major advertising campaign that emphasized how the new Chiquita bananas are so special that they are handled with tender loving care.

Before we left, the ambassador promised to go to Lepaterigue for a visit and offered money for our projects (about two hundred dollars from some kind of discretionary budget) if it would do good for our town. As we were departing, he invited us all to come to his residence that evening for "Cokes and beer." We gladly accepted – and it turned out to be one of the highlights of our weekend (in more ways than one!)

The residence sits way up on top of a hill and looks out over the city – beautiful at night. The Embassy residence is very elegant on a hill –

too extravagant to be appropriate in such a poor country. Mrs. Jova, British accent and all, showed us around the main floor of their residence – apologizing for the disarray of their things "due to our having just moved in." She is a very likeable, friendly – not at all stuffy – person, and we were all impressed. Drinks and hors d' oeuvres were served and we spent a delightful two hours there.

In the afternoon, we all went to see Fernando Montez, a young lawyer and a graduate of Texas A&M in agriculture. He is part of the recently organized Christian Democrats. They are promoting the Scandinavian style of government. He is a definitely an up-and-coming young man, who has a lot of good ideas for the how the people of Honduras can improve themselves. He is fortunate because he has the money with which to back many of his projects, such as teaching the people how to improve their land and to produce better crops and teaching them the basis of various political parties (Communism, Capitalism, Democracy). He explained to us how he got his start in politics in the city university and a little about his political hopes for the future. We came away very impressed and hope he succeeds. Jaquith seems to think that in about ten years he will be President of Honduras

In the evening – after the Ambassador's, we toured the night spots (that is, we enjoyed bar hopping).

Sunday, July 18

This morning was for sightseeing – in three different groups due to a communications SNAFU. Mainly we visited two towns that had hosted Cornell teams in the two prior years. As we passed through Santa Ana, we were stopped by a group that had stretched a rope across the road and made a "voluntary" contribution to a fund for celebrating the saint's day before they would lower the rope.

The Cornell Central America project started in Guatemala. Two years ago it expanded into Honduras. The first team stayed in Ojojona, which is a weekend resort for Tegucigalpa. It is just eight kilometers off the paved road connecting the capital with the Pan-American Highway. Our guide pointed out two Nationalist ex-Presidents sitting near the only Cadillac I've seen in Honduras. Both are Nationalist; one a ninety year old ex-long term dictator. The Cornell team lived in relative luxury, staying in apartments loaned by upper class Tegucigalpans. They initiated work that led to a new six grade school supported by the Alliance. The town also has a full time Alliance Clinic and a "J.F.K." kindergarten.

At La Venta, the site of one of last year's teams, everyone bought necklaces made from local seed pods. The necklaces were the product of a cooperative organized by a Peace Corps volunteer. This town also has a "J.F.K." Center, which gets a once a week visit by an Alliance doctor. In all of our political conversations with locals, Kennedy is admired, respected or even adored and seen as making a change from the tradition of exploitive, "gun boat diplomacy" treatment of Central America. For the most part, Lyndon Johnson is an unknown. I was discouraged by our visit to La Venta, because as far as I could ascertain, the Cornell team had no real effect on the town. One year later, it was as if they had never been there.

To a Milparadan, both places looked rich and well-developed.

In the afternoon, we had a choice between rest and a football (soccer) game. I chose the game. We took a local bus to the stadium in Comaguela. Comaguela is connected to Tegucigalpa by three bridges. The only traffic light is on the Comaguela side of the main bridge. (It is turned off at night.) The stadium is a large, beautiful new structure. It is part of a massive development program of the last Liberal government. The nearby large maternity hospital was completed almost two years ago but it has never opened for use; it remains surrounded by a chain link fence. There is talk of converting it to a general hospital, but only talk. There is a large empty area on the other side of the stadium which had been cleared for other developments that never got off the ground. Just beyond that is a true slum; shacks made of corrugated iron sheets and scrap wood.

Today's game Tegucigalpa vs. San Pedro Sula was relatively mild. They still talk about the "soccer war" between Honduras and El Salvador which was set off by a disputed call in a game between the two national teams and escalated into a series of border skirmishes between their armies. The new stadium has a moat between the seats and the field to prevent fan violence from reaching the field. Tickets cost 1.05 Lempira (fifty-three cents) for seats in the sun and 1.75 Lempira for the shady side. We were accosted by kids outside begging money, ostensibly to get in to see the game. Inside vendors were selling cigarettes singly, along with a variety of snacks that did not look sanitary.

We splurged tonight and had steak dinners out of our personal funds at the Lincoln Hotel. The Lincoln is the premier hotel in Tegucigalpa that caters mostly to rich gringos. Juan had tracked down the fares for our return trip. The one hour flight leaves in the early afternoon and costs L25.00 ($12.50) plus another couple of bucks for a shared ride to the airport. The cheapest option is a converted truck with backless wood benches in the back (L5.00), followed by L6.00 for a school bus, or L7.00 for a VW *busito*. The rest of the team opted for the flight and went off to see "The Sound of Music." I'm low on spending money, so I chose the better bus ride. I'm going to bed now because my bus is scheduled to leave at 2:00am.

Monday, July 19

     I got up at 1:30 am for a 2:00 bus which picked up each passenger at his door, so it didn't get out of Tegucigalpa until 3:30 am. (At least this one had working headlights.) We only had nine passengers, so the crowding was not bad. From then on, it was a pleasant ride, much better than the way up on Friday. I got off the bus at Chamelecon (where the road to Quimistan joins the San Pedro highway) at 10:30am and got to Quimistan on two hitches (with only minimal waits). I ate a big lunch at Castillo's. My one Lempira (fifty cents) got me a small bowl of soup, a full plate with meat, rice, beans, and sweet potato, along with tortillas, coffee and a beer. (I skipped the fresh vegetable salad included in the price.)

     I walked back to Milparada, arriving at 1:30 pm. I had saved several hours by not riding all the way into San Pedro and transferring to the Quimistan bus. It doesn't make a lot of sense from an objective point of view, but Milparada looks better than any place I saw on the trip. I am back home.

     Everybody seemed surprised to see me. Since I arrived alone, they naturally assumed that the others had decided not to return (and probably figured that I had come just to pick up our baggage). I spent most of the afternoon and evening writing my by now infamous notes and chatting with townspeople, mostly reassuring them: "Yes, the others will come. Of course, I came back."

     I also wrote a letter home:

Monday, Mid July

Dear family,

When it rains here, it pours. I wouldn't be surprised if we are getting as much here today as Phoenix gets in a year. We've only got three real leaks in our roof, but when it comes down especially hard, occasional drops splash through all over. We are getting rain two or three times a week, usually not quite as hard or long as today. It's hot from about 9 until 2:30 when the clouds build up. If it doesn't rain, the evenings are pleasant. After a rain, it gets cold enough at night to use a blanket.

I got back from our trip to Tegucigalpa today. It was an extremely worthwhile educational trip, but I'm glad to be back home. We all went by bus, a scenic but slow trip since most of the road between Pedro and Tegucigalpa (the two biggest cities in Honduras) is about as good as the old Mingus Mountain road. There were 47 passengers (and a piano blocking the emergency exit) in an old school bus designed for 36. (As usual, I made friends with a boy of the bus and had a great time talking with him.) All the others decided to fly back, but I got up at 1:30 this morning, caught a good busito to Chamelecon and hitched rides from two Jeeps to Quimistan where I ate lunch, then I got an oxcart ride half-way here and walked the rest. Trip (straight line distance well under 100 miles) took only 12 hours (vs. 17 hours to get the other way) If you're worried about hitchhiking, relax, it's perfectly safe for campesinos and extremely easy for gringos, and I'm in both boats. The townspeople were very happy to see me. Many were afraid that we weren't coming back. The others were supposed to arrive between 7 & 8 and it's now past 9. If they don't make it in an hour or so, I'll probably have to be a one man team tomorrow.

Thank you Loie, Mom and Dad for the letters. In answer to the question of food, I think my last letter shows we are doing well. The only problem is that we're heavy to starch, meat is virtually unavailable and in order to have a couple of eggs apiece for breakfast, we have to buy up the entire town's supply for at least two days.

I've got a lot more to say, but I'm so tired I can't see straight.

Hasta luego,

The rest of the team spent the morning walking around Tegucigalpa and flew back to San Pedro after lunch. The actual flight was only 30 minutes. Juan and Doug each took a pillow from the plane for use here. In typical Honduran fashion, the Pinalejo *busito* they hired was two hours late, so they relaxed in Jackie's for the remainder of the time. After stopping at Nelly's, they arrived home at 10:00 pm, waking me up. Their arrival disrupted Pedro and his woman, who were enjoying the privacy of being alone in the girls' house.

Tuesday, July 20

At 7:00 we were all up and ready to go. Breakfast was the usual ration of oatmeal. We now have about twenty-five days to finish our *comedor*, finish building the desks and make the furniture for the *comedor*.

Happy to be back home, we worked all morning long laying and leveling the foundation for the building. Our burst of enthusiasm didn't last long. After two or three hours, those of us working on the *comedor* were ready to quit. The heat was intolerable and our energy was rapidly diminishing. The girls continued washing, a hard task and harder than usual since we had more than the normal load after the trip. While Trinchi, Mary and Melissa washed, I joined Sue and we continued with desk building (in the shade of the boys' house. We had had some trouble with them in the beginning, but I think we have now mastered the art of assembling CARE desks, a sturdy design, but imperfectly cut and made out of green, warped wood.

Melissa and Mary both continue to be very active in the health program, and the town has been very receptive to their ministrations and good will. Now they are making notes to send home with the school children tomorrow in another attempt to draw an audience to a health class.

The afternoon rain cooled things off, and also brought a pleasant surprise. Pedro had fixed all the leaks in the roof of the girl's house while we were in Tegucigalpa. There were no drips to catch during our evening meal.

Our after dinner discussion centered on the question: "What could Milparada do with $200?" (The question was raised by the Ambassador's offer). We could use the money, if we really get it. Our ideas:

1)	Start a producers' cooperative that would have the 400 *Lempiras* as initial capital and would buy the town's corn at the lowest price time in the market. They usually sell this corn at a disadvantage to middle men who sell it back to them at higher prices. The corn bought by the cooperative would provide the small farmer with money when prices are lowest by buying corn, but keeping the money in the community and splitting the profits when sold at higher prices. The problem would be that much more than two hundred dollars would be needed to buy all the local corn. Estimates are that the total crop would fetch up to 3,000 *Lempiras* – plus capital would be needed for storage bins.
2)	A credit cooperative could be started with this small amount of capital. As above, interest would be charged for loans

that would range from ten to twenty-five *Lempiras*. This would be very good for the small farmer who does not own the land he works (so cannot qualify for a bank loan from the Alliance for Progress). These farmers do not want to borrow five hundred *Lempiras*, just enough to buy higher quality seed at the start of planting season.

3)   A small industry could be started -- perhaps building bricks that could be sold in the district with cooperative voluntary work. The profits would go to a communal fund. Machinery for making the bricks could be obtained through CARE.

4)   Buy some steel plows (four to eight) to be loaned by the community. This is probably the weakest of these projects. I am not sure that this would make a lasting change and it would not represent an investment from which interest could be obtained. Also, the steel plows wouldn't help the poorest farmers whose plots are on the steep hillsides.

I don't think we have enough time left to implement any of these programs this summer. Maybe next year's team will be able to follow up on the offer. It is interesting and difficult to try to think of practical things that a team like us could do to help the community really develop economically.

Team morale seems to be at an all-time high. I think that's partly due to the short time remaining in which we have so much to accomplish, and partly due to the perspective we have gained by seeing more of the country. Our cooking has improved by leaps and bounds. Melissa deserves a special mention in this respect.

Wednesday, July 21

Wednesday nothing happened out of the ordinary.

Instead of writing about our routine again, I can give the preliminary results of a research project I am doing. I took a course in Social Psychology last semester and greatly enjoyed both the course and the professor. So I arranged to do an independent study course with him for the next semester, with the goal of trying out some of the sociometric techniques this summer to see if they could add to my understanding of the villagers. While our project is primarily devoted to community development work, the professor agreed that it provided an excellent opportunity for research, in some respects better than a formal "research project".

This particular project, finding factors which correlate with the status of the townspeople, was chosen with two goals in mind: 1) To help people on community development projects in Latin America pick out the people in a village with influence fairly quickly and easily, and 2) To compare the correlates of status in Latin America with those in the United States.

My subjects are the nine boys in the second and third grades (taught as a combined class) in the village. This group was chosen for both practical and theoretical reasons. They were the easiest group to study, since I had become a friend of each of the boys before doing the data collection, and since their normal playground was right in front of our house. The two main theoretical advantages were that, while our programs involve individual adults, we generally work with the boys as a group through the school, therefore their status system is less likely to have been altered by their degree of association with us. Also because of the individualistic culture of the villagers, the schoolboys are practically the only stable, defined small group in town, other than individual families. The girls in the class are not included because they mostly stayed at home outside of school hours, so I have had very little opportunity to get to know them individually. That shouldn't hurt the data because there is virtually no interaction between them and the boys outside of the classroom.

The boys represent a good cross-section of the town's families. Nevertheless, because of the makeup of the village, they form a fairly homogenous group. All the boys are *mestizos*, part Indian, part white, but the percentages vary. All plan to work in the fields after third grade, all are nominally Catholics, and all are poor. They have a very small world; only two have ever been to San Pedro Sula, the nearest city of any size. Their ages vary from nine to fifteen.

Victor Dubon is twelve years old, in third grade, and easily the best dressed kid in town (and the only one with shoes and socks). He owns the only bicycle I've seen in town (other than the one the Rafael loaned us). His family owns the small general store and a few head of cattle, in addition to farming. He has two little brothers. Although he enjoys playing soccer, he often quits if asked to play barefooted like everyone else. He is the custodian of the soccer ball that Tutico (from last year's team) gave them. He is a spunky wrestler, self-identified tough guy. He is temperamental, and especially does not like to lose any game.   Victor does well in school, even though his attendance is poor and he is often inattentive when he is there, probably out of boredom. He doesn't participate in the twice a week craft class of weaving baskets. Still, he is the teacher's pet. Victor has been to San Pedro Sula once for less than a day and liked it because it is so big. He is not interested in learning English or continuing school. He is ready to work in the fields next year.

Nicolas Hernandez is eleven and in third grade. He was born in El Salvador. He had chicken pox when we arrived; that didn't affect his school attendance – he came even while the rash was active. He lives with his mother, her new man and their three small daughters. He has not seen his own father in four years. He told me that his father lives in San Pedro with a new wife and has a job cutting trees. He is quiet, a good student – especially at reading. He passed the second grade completion test with distinction. Nico is highly sensitive to the emotions of other people, easily the most empathetic child in town. Yet, he consciously "acts macho" – a man must be tough. Nico dreams of becoming a schoolteacher, but the chances of his completing the necessary eight years of school are very slim. (He will have to walk over an hour each way to go to Pinalejo, the closest school that goes beyond third grade – and will have to work in the fields during the school year.) His clothes are thoroughly patched. He has shoes, but they hurt his feet, so goes barefoot most of the time. He often has nothing to eat at lunch time. He states that he is a Catholic, but has never been in a church nor seen a priest. He spends a lot of time with our team. He is interested in English and picks up the words quickly. Nico likes to listen to the radio for news and "love notices."

Roberto Escalon is also eleven years old and in the third grade. He is the apparent leader of the group. He usually takes the initiative in organizing soccer games, etc. (He came up early on and asked me "When are you going to teach us English?" After I demurred, he got the other kids and the school teacher to talk me into giving a couple of lessons.) He hates to be left out of any group activity. When he had a sore, cut foot, he got tears in his eyes when I told him he shouldn't play soccer that day – but brightened up quickly when I backed down. He lives with his mother and four younger siblings (one brother and three sisters). The family lives in a small thatched hut (the two beds crowd the bedroom). His father lives in the village, but in a different house with another woman.   Both households live off a five *manzana* (nine acre) plot right behind his house. His mother works in the *Tobacalera* in Quimistan. Roberto is fluent with the multiplication table, names and values of all the different Central American monetary units, and could name the President of Honduras. When asked why he thought I had come here, he replied, "To help the country".

"What are you going to do next year?"

"I am going to the United States."

"Really?"

"I will be a worker."

Roberto is sensitive; his feelings are easily hurt. He is also accident prone, getting lots of minor injuries. I think part of that problem is the result of his trying too hard to be a man too soon. When we were gathering rocks for the foundation he would pick out the biggest ones he could find and throw them onto the oxcart. He borrowed some books from us and read them at home. He told me the stories they contained when he returned them.

Antonio Cruz, fourteen years old and in third grade, is the middle of nine kids (by two fathers) in a poor (even by local standards) family. His clothes are ragged and usually dirty. He does fairly well in school, considering that he often has to skip class to do chores. He is the tallest boy in the school, but quite skinny. While the students were preparing the garden, he stood out as a hard worker, vigorously wielding a pickax. Antonio spends a lot of time playing with the younger children, especially "buttons" (a game kind of like tiddly winks). He showed me the collection of two hundred buttons he has won. He does most of the household chores for his family. He started taking water from our tap the first day it was available; he never asked permission even though it is clearly within our back yard and only a few steps closer to his house than the tap in the plaza. Antonio has firmly attached himself to our team. He frequently offers to help us with menial chores and is delighted if he is given a penny for his efforts. He has expressed almost no curiosity or interest in anything outside of his daily existence. When I asked about his plans for next year, the answer was simply, "I will work my field." When I asked about friends, he said he doesn't have any. Sadly, he feels left out. None of the other boys named him as a friend, so his perception is accurate.

Victoriano Gomez, fifteen and in the second grade, is loud and boisterous. He is quick to volunteer answers in class (with the self-confidence that comes from having heard the questions many times before). Although officially in the second grade (he has never passed the final exam), about half the time he works on the third grade assignments. Toriano is from another one of the poorer families, and is constantly seeking attention. Since free government education stops at the age of fifteen, he will never go to third grade. He is in an ambiguous social situation; all the other boys of his age are out working in the fields. He doesn't quite fit in with his younger classmates. Still he is generally happy.

Oscar Machado, eleven and in third grade with two younger brothers, is Antonio's son. Oscar is intelligent, well-dressed (but barefooted), fairly quiet, and a terribly sweet and nice guy. He has been to San Pedro Sula, but did not like it. He doesn't know who the President of Honduras is, but has picked up a bit of world knowledge from listening to the radio with his father. For example, he could tell me about Vietnam: "There are two, one North and one South. There's a war there. It has something to do with Cuba." He claims to be able to recognize gringos because they are soft spoken. He likes school, but says that "the others only go because they want to learn, but they don't enjoy it." He went to the doctor at the Alliance for Progress four times in the last year, when he was sick. Oscar frequently volunteers to help our team members with chores.

David Machado, nine and in the second grade, is Oscar's little brother. HE is the shortest boy in the group. He resembles Oscar in many ways, but is louder and more active. He is the leader of the younger boys.

Lionel Padilla, nine and in the second grade, is shy but friendly. When I hang out with some of the boys in the plaza, he almost always comes over and stands quietly on the edge of the group. He is physically petite. He is a poor student, barely able to read. His family is relatively well off. He is Eduardo DuBon's son. He spends a lot of time playing with his toddler brother.

Rubin Martin is nine years old and in second grade. He is small for his age, even by local standards. He is extremely shy and quiet.

The basic procedure was to list the boys in rank order on the basis of various observable criteria. After all these scales were constructed, I interviewed each boy, asking about who they liked and disliked and used that information to make a status rating. The observable criteria are:

Age: Straight physical age, learned by asking each boy.

School Performance: The teacher rated the boys for me. This was a statement about the amount of knowledge shown on tests, and not an estimate of intelligence.

Dress: Based on personal observation. This took in account the quality (store-bought vs. homemade from flour sacks), the amount of patching (or degree of raggedness) and the cleanliness of the garments.

Family Wealth: Another judgment call I made mostly on the basis of any luxuries (like a radio) owned by the family, the amount of livestock (mostly chickens, a few pigs), tile v. straw roofs, household furnishings (particularly the number of people per bed), and the amount of land farmed.

Amount of Time Voluntarily Spent with our Team: simply based on the amount of time the kids spent helping us, hindering us, talking with us, and just gaping at us.

Time with Elders: The observations for this were based mostly on who participated in the bull sessions in the plaza after the men came in from the fields, and on who played soccer with the teenagers and young men vs. who watched those games vs. who wasn't there.

Time with Younger Boys: based almost entirely on the extent to which the boys participated in various forms of play (other than soccer) with the younger children.

Soccer Ability: I rated this by observing the soccer games among only the school boy held during school recess. Since I often play goalie, I've been in an excellent position to judge their relative abilities.

Extrovertedness: – The boys were rated from exhibitionist, through outgoing and friendly, and so on down to shy and withdrawn.

Displayed Initiative: Who actually started the various group activities? Especially heavy weight was given to initiating games, etc. involving all, or most of, the group, but initiative shown in other groups, and in doing things alone were considered as tie breakers.

Estimated Status: As a reality check, I made a personal estimate of the relative amount of esteem and/or respect received by each boy while the group was together.

To create a sociogram and scale of actual status, I asked each of the boys who his three best friends were, if there was somebody in school they didn't like and if so whom. The questions were asked in private conversations spread out over the past week. In seven cases, the questions were brought up in a normal conversation, whenever I happened to be alone with one of the boys. Since I'm always asking them some question or another, the boys didn't ascribe any particular importance to new ones. They answered quite readily (somewhat to my surprise). The only problem was that most of the boys, although asked to name three friends, would only identify one or two. When pressed, they said either: "The rest are equal" or "I don't have any other friends." My relationship with the last two boys is weaker, so I had to ask them to come and talk to me about school. After a few preliminary questions about the subjects and the teachers, I asked about their friends. Davio answered nicely, but Rubin didn't respond until the question was changed to "Of the boys in school, who do you like, and which ones don't you like?" He gave a slow roll-call vote: "I like Davio . . . and Victor . . ."

"What about Roberto?"

"I don't like him, he fights . . . I don't like Antonio either . . . but I like Oscar ..."

Each boy was assigned a score equal to the number of friendship choices received minus the number of rejections received. Victor and Roberto came out on top, with Antonio clearly at the bottom.

When I get back to campus, I'll do the formal calculations of correlation coefficients between this score and the rankings on each of the independent variables. However, some patterns are clear without running the statistics. My estimate of their status ranking was almost identical to the calculated score. That relieves some doubts I had about whether the technique is valid.

Five factors appear to be closely tied to the status scores. They can be divided into two clusters. Soccer Ability, Time Spent with Elders, and Time Spent with Youngsters (the less the better) make up one cluster. Dress and Family Wealth are the second cluster. This latter is no surprise, but it is interesting to note that dress is a much better indicator of effective affluence than was actual wealth. Of the first group, soccer ability is probably the central factor. Since the boys are not yet workers, their principal opportunity to gain admittance into the group of teenagers and young men is through playing soccer with them. Similarly, those who can't play soccer well are more apt to spend their time playing other games with the smaller children, where they can come out on top. For example, Antonio, who is the worst soccer player in the third grade, spends much more time with the small fry than any other third grader; he is the champion of "*botones*".

There doesn't appear to be any connection between a boy's performance in school and his status with his peers. That matches up with my own memories of grade school.

So what are the implications for a community development worker looking for potential leaders in a small Latin American village? First, to a large extent, he can trust his eyes: the neat, well-dressed man is probably a high status individual. Beyond this, there appears to be a negative correlation between status and extrovertedness and the amount of time spent with our team. That would indicate that one should be especially cautious about putting that nice-fellow-who-shows-you-around-town-and-offers-all-kinds-of-help into a leadership position. There is a good chance that he is trying to improve his low status by being associated with the rich and powerful outsider. Also, I didn't see any relationship between the status score and displayed initiative, which would indicate that there is a good possibility that the most influential men in town will not be among the currently outspoken.

Thursday, July 22

While nothing exciting happened on Wednesday, Wednesnight was a different was a different story. Something woke me up about 3:15am. Since I quite naturally itched all over, I applied some Calamine lotion and lay there and listened. I heard screams coming from next door and got up to see what was going on. Trinchi let me in the front door, she was dressed in a bathrobe, curlers and combat boots. Melissa, suitably robed, was standing on the bench. Sue was peering beneath the curtain from the safety of her cot. Mary undoubtedly had the covers pulled up tight. It seems that some giant rodent had been eating penicillin mold off the bread and washing it down with Kool-Aid. He'd also sampled a bit of rat poison and crawled into the corner of the kitchen. Anyhow, Ed picked up a length of pipe and cautiously approached the corner from which the strange sounds were emanating. A flashlight did not reveal the suspect. After a short conference, we decided to let the poison finish it off and went back to bed. Sue did not get back to sleep. With this morning's light, we still can't find the rat, or whatever it was.

Today was a letdown – very normal , EXCEPT: We finally had success in holding a class for mothers – health, first-aid and nutrition. In a typically American way, Melissa had sent out notes with all the school children; in a surprising way, it worked and seventeen mothers showed up for the meeting. With all of them crowded into the girls' house (a couple leaning through the front door), Melissa and Mary gave a lesson in Spanish utilizing material developed by Peace Corps workers for such classes. The first class was how to boil water for drinking purposes and maintain its purity, and secondly, how to observe proper body hygiene.

This afternoon, I took a walk along a secondary trail leading out of the other side of town. Just past the river, I came across the graveyard. The graves were marked by wooden crosses, almost hidden by weeds. Most of the crosses were just two pieces of rough wood nailed together; only a few were whitewashed. Three of the graves had extremely wilted wreaths lying on them. We haven't had any deaths in town since we've been here. Though I am curious about their funerals, I'd rather not have to experience one.

I encountered a few isolated houses scattered near this path. I only saw one person, a woman baking an earthen jar. The jar was sitting on the ground with a slow burning, smoky fire built over it. She was using a surprisingly large amount of wood for just one pot.

A little farther on, the vegetation turned to true forest with pine trees growing on the side of the mountain and very little undergrowth other than grass. It looked like a park. The next section was nothing but charred stumps. The lumber company does no reforestation. After clear cutting an area and extracting the logs, they just burn the scrap and move on. Mr. Fisher had told us that at the rate things are going, the forests will be depleted in another fifteen years.

We are a united team in spirit, but not in our habits. We have become accustomed to each others personal quirks and styles. Ed wakes up promptly and is immediately ready to face the day; the rest of the boys start the day with a grumble and straggle to breakfast. Ed is also our neatnik. He complains if he gets a spot on his pants. In contrast, I get teased about becoming attached (literally) to my "Cuban Army" work shirt. I actually alternate between identical long sleeve khaki shirts, and wash them regularly. Being from the desert, I know that they are cooler (well, less hot) than other colors and provide good protections against sunburn while reducing the area exposed to bug bites. Ed and Doug often work shirtless, wanting to return to New York with a great tan. All of the local men and boys wear short sleeve whitish shirts and long pants; I have never seen any of them without a shirt on. I'm not in on the ladies' gossip, so I don't know whether they are scandalized or attracted to Doug's and Ed's exposed muscular torsos.

Juan and Doug regularly argue about how to do the next construction task and about the time they reach agreement, Antonio comes along with a completely different method. Pedro always stops by at some point during the day to visit, greeting us with *"Mucho trabajo"* (A lot of work). If Don Lelo is with us, he finishes four cups of coffee while talking through a meal.

Mary is our most dedicated homemaker, she usually sets the table for lunch regardless of who the day's cooks are. Mary and Sue take a daily nap.

In the evening, Melissa reads the Bible the reads or re-reads her pile of mail, while Mary writes more letters. Ed fiddles with (studies) bugs. Doug fiddles with the radio, trying to get a station other than Radio Havana or the BBC. The BBC provides us our daily update on world news. I work on my notes and our team financial ledger. Even though we aren't being extravagant by a long shot, at the rate we are spending, we will run out of money before our final week. Nobody else seems to care about that. Juan assures us that somehow it will all work out fine.

July 23 (written the next day)

This was at least a day and a half. I think we all grew a little bit today. As a team, we all played a part in a drama that probably saved two lives.

The day surely had begun normally: breakfast followed by work on the *comedor* and desks. Melissa and Mary expected a second good health class today, but no women came. Two or three faithful and outstanding women were willing and did continue to come. They explained that the other women were just too lazy and occupied with other things to be bothered. Melissa tried to rule out the occupation with other things by questioning the women as to which hour of the day would suit them best, but it was to no avail. I suspect that given the limited firewood and pots in most of the houses, along with the amount of time required, they think that boiling all their water is impractical, as well as unnecessary. The nurses' limited Spanish is also a problem.

Mary made some delicious banana bread for lunch. At the end of lunch, our minds were a thousand miles away, talking about Cornell. Melissa was on her cot reading about the birth of Samuel in the Bible, when who should arrive at the door but one of our friends who was expecting. (She already has given birth to five children – the last two by Caesarean). Her words were: "The time has come." Labor pains had started the day before at about 6:00pm. That brought us back to the present – chopping fire wood, starting to boil water and collecting clean towels. Sue's cot had, covered with Mary's poncho, became the senora's "labor room." From Melissa's judgment, there was a good chance that this baby would require a C-section as well. So I was dispatched to Quimistan on the bicycle. I got there in fifteen minutes, but had trouble finding help. The Amigos are no longer in town and the Alliance Mobile Health team had gone to San Pedro Sula for a couple of days. That left Blanca, the Alliance nurse. She told me, "I can't leave the clinic . . . I can't treat her unless you have a house where she can stay in Quimistan for a few days." The only reachable medical resource was the former United Fruit lab technician (who we privately refer to as a quack). I reluctantly called on him, since at least he has a Jeep.

His "hospital" was crowded and dirty – a bunch of patients sharing a single large ward, ventilated by open space between the top of the walls and the roof, allowing lots of flies in. Only a few of the cots had mosquito nets over them. The atmosphere, equipment and odors seemed like a poorly-run dog pound. The "doctor" was going from patient to patient, talking to one while changing the bandages on a patient in the next cot. There were hypodermics lying around uncovered; he picked one up, refilled it and gave a shot without sterilization. I would have turned around and

98

gone back, admitting my mission had failed, but his wife came up next to me and asked why I had come. The "doctor" soon joined us. When I told him a woman who had two previous Caesarean deliveries was about to need another one, he said that was very dangerous. He grabbed his black bag and drove me and his wife back to Milparada.

He opened the black suitcase and pulled out its contents, one white rag with which he cleaned his hands. His examination told him that she might need a couple of days to be ready to deliver and at best we should give her quinine to speed things up. (It was now about 2:00pm.) He said he would return at 8:00 tonight to try to get that baby out with a small incision, if need be. "Just one little cut, like this, and it opens right up - - very easy." This did not match his earlier comments to me on how dangerous the third Caesarian was.

At this point, none of us were happy with the situation but didn't have any good alternatives to offer. At least there seemed to be some time left before the baby arrived.

So Ed and Juan went back to Quimistan with the lab technician. Ed got the quinine pills and cycled back in record time. Juan stayed in Quimistan and talked to Blanca, asking her if the "doctor" would be qualified to do the operation. The answer was a sharp "No." They could not handle it at the Alliance clinic either. It could only be done at San Pedro Sula.

When Juan had gone to get the mail this morning he had met a rich Costa Rican merchant, Senor Raul Fernandez, who currently lives in Quimistan. After learning that they were fellow countrymen and listening to Juan's description of what we were doing, he made an offer of the use of his car in case we ever needed it. Once again, we had a stroke of luck in a time of need. He needed his Jeep later tonight but would let Juan use it to go to Cofradia and summon Nelly Duarte with her pickup truck to take the woman to San Pedro. Juan hasn't driven for two years, so he walked/ran back to Milparada to get an experienced Jeep driver.

Doug had experience driving Jeeps on mountain trails last summer so he was elected to go back with Juan and do the driving. Around 5:00pm, they have Raul's Jeep and are on their way to Cofradia. Halfway there a truck threw a rather large stone in the air that hit the Jeep's steering mechanism, the wheels locked and the Jeep veered sharply left. They came to a stop just off the side of the road, looked the Jeep over and drove it around a little bit before deciding that no serious harm had been done. They got to Cofradia a little before Nelly and her father came in from their ranch. They unloaded their truck. Doug drove the pickup and Juan drove the Jeep. They made it back safely to Quimistan, dropped off the Jeep and drove on to Milparada.

The rest of the team kept watch, timed the labor pains and half-heartedly prepared and ate dinner. How relieved we all were that Juan and Doug got back before the Lab Technician. By this time (7:15 pm), a crowd was beginning to gather at our door. The mother-to-be and Melissa, clutching a bag with "delivery supplies", climbed into the truck with Doug and headed out to San Pedro. Off they jounced, with Doug assuring Melissa that it would be all right and that we had made the right choice in whisking the woman away from our quack friend's incompetent hands. They passed him on the road, but he didn't show any signs of recognizing the truck.

Doug handled the rough road with due haste. In one hour, they reached the edge of San Pedro (compared to the two-and-a-half hours of the normal bus ride). Our patient had fared well on the trip but was getting a bit "worse for wear" about then. They stopped at Bondano's clinic and were directed to the Leonardo Martinez government hospital. Some soldiers met them at the door and soon brought out a stretcher. There was some confusion as to whether Doug was the father or a doctor, or just who. The admission officer started off by asking what was wrong with this woman, lying before him on a stretcher. Then off to the maternity ward. In a few minutes, a doctor came out to explain that the examination revealed that the baby was alive. They would now X-ray to determine whether a Caesarian would be necessary or not. At any rate, it would be another two hours or more. So feeling like a great burden was lifted, they returned to the truck and arrived back at Nelly's in Cofradia at 11:30 pm. Poor Nelly greeted them royally and insisted that they sleep over.

Meanwhile, the local "doctor" arrived in Milparada at 8:05, ready to see the patient. The conversation went as follows: First he asked how the patient was. Juan told him that the situation had worsened and we had decided to send her to San Pedro Sula. The man was very obviously upset. Juan tried to calm the storm somewhat, but could not get him to talk about anything else. He kept saying: "It was very bad, you send her away, we should have fought to the very end, until we met death or saved the baby or the mother . . . If she dies, well, tomorrow there will be another case like it and maybe then we can save the patient ... We should have treated her here, they won't be able to do anything at San Pedro and if she dies, what difference does it make for the poor devil to die in San Pedro or here? Better for her to die in Milparada, isn't it? You shouldn't have given up, you have lost the battle. We must face the problems and not run away from them."

We did not agree with him, but remembering that he is probably in fact the only half qualified person within miles, from his point of view, he was quite right. We may have won a battle today, but we haven't accomplished much in the larger war. The villagers' health problems will continue. What will happen to them when the gringos leave?

Tonight, the rat hunt continued keeping the other girls quite awake. We set out a couple of baited traps before retiring. Sue saw the rat tonight, avoided screaming and described it as smallish, brown and quite intelligent (in his ability to avoid getting caught or trapped).

Saturday, July 24

Today was a bit anticlimactic after yesterday's hair-raiser. Doug and Melissa went back to San Pedro for our shopping and determined that the mother and baby came through okay. (Our baby was delivered with forceps. The Caesarian not needed.) They had lunch with Nelly in Cofradia and waited for the expected 1:00pm arrival of Don Lelo until 4:00pm before leaving without him. We got a bigger and later rainstorm than usual, and Nelly's truck got stuck in the mud where the road goes through the river. With Doug and Melissa pushing and getting covered with mud, they got free.

Don Lelo did show up, shortly after Nelly, and brought us some fresh bread and four live chickens for dinner. Ed started off to get the hatchet to cut off their heads (as we did in our training). Lelo shook his head and said that wasn't the right way to do it. He handed each of the boys a chicken, held by the legs. With appropriate gestures, he told us the best way to kill a chicken is to firmly hold it under your arm, grab the back of its neck with the other hand and give a quick, twisting snap. Doing it his way, I only felt a short, strong spasm from the body when I heard its neck break. I could then reach down to grab its legs and dunk it into the pot of boiling water to get it ready to pluck. This was much better than the beheading and watching the body "run around like a chicken with its head cut off."

Meanwhile, today we completed the preparation of the *comedor* floor. We spread, leveled and tamped down a layer of sand. Now it is ready for us to start pouring the nine-inch-thick cement slab - if only the cement would arrive. Also, the school children have finished preparing their garden. It is neat rows of furrows, freshly planted with a variety of vegetable seeds.

Tomorrow the members of the Rotary Club are coming to look over our project. Everyone is anxiously awaiting their arrival and hope that they will be favorably impressed by our accomplishments. Since they are footing the bill for the materials we still need, their approval is critical. As we neatened up the woodpile in anticipation of their visit, we killed two more small velvet snakes.

After dinner, Pedro came over to join our nightly "bull session." During this conversation, the rat was spotted running along a ceiling beam. So we reset the trap before going to bed.

Sunday, July 25

The morning got off to a great start. The rat was dead in the trap, with his neck broken. Doug spotted another rat outside, next to the backdoor and immediately killed it with a quick blow from a piece of pipe. Two down, and an unknown number to go.

The Rotary members pulled in around 10:30am. We were all glad to see them, (and the load of cement that came with them) even though only three members showed up, along with a representative of *La Prensa*. He took notes and pictures for a feature story on us. Rafael Davila had gotten up at 6 am (after partying until 3:00am) to come. He was accompanied by Jorge Larach and Armando Gutierrez, who has been skeptical about our project. We also met Carlos Izagurre, a young man from Quimistan who will be going to a college in Massachusetts, thanks to the family of one of last year's Cornell team.

Don Lelo had called a town meeting in order to present Milparada and the Rotarians to each other. The local turnout was strong – my head count was one hundred and fifteen people. Pedro opened the ceremony in front of the school with appropriate words about mutual understanding between Cornell and Honduras, then Armando Gutierrez spoke for the Rotary. His words were polite, but non-committal. Of course, Don Lelo had something to say. After the meeting, picture taking and a brief tour, we retired to our house, squeezing fifteen people around our table for a delicious lunch, supplied by the Rotarians.

It appears that the day was a real success. All the visitors showed a real interest in our work and in the whole philosophy of our program. They now have a real image of what we have done and the problems of the village. It felt like a real Sunday, with the midday feast and all. After all the guests left, we relaxed: resting, reading, listening to the radio, walking in the rain.

I took shelter from the heaviest part of the rain in Eduardo DuBon's house/store. Eduardo is thirty-four and looks younger, which is rare in these parts. He is the acknowledged village carpenter. He is illiterate, but learning to read from the team. He learns fast and has been studying a lot on his own. He is fascinated by books and writing.

He acts like one of the schoolboys when he is around the team. Eduardo told me that he had never attended school because his family had been too poor with five kids. Now he has a corn field on good bottom land. His house is larger than most – the bedroom has three beds (wood frames with rope weave covered by a straw mattress) and a hammock in one corner. The central room serves as the store. Today the stock consists of one bag of rice, one bag of flour, one bag of sugar, and a shelf with three five-pound bags of coffee, some chewing gum and some cigarettes, and three cases of empty pop and beer bottles. (I have never seen a full bottle here.) The shelf also holds his portable record player (which uses two flashlight batteries) and a stack of about ten 45 rpm records. A table and bench are against one wall and a stool is near the door. None of furniture has ever been varnished or painted. Four rough planks are placed across the ceiling beams for storage. Most of that storage is for baskets of corn. At this time of year, most of the baskets are empty. The kitchen appears to be amply supplied with utensils. I also saw a couple of toads in the house.

Eduardo's "wife" is a very Indian looking lady of about twenty-eight. Her skin is wrinkled from time in the sun and she has frayed, stringy black hair. She wears a nice looking dress, but doesn't button the top. Her parents, who are old but still healthy, sleep in the kitchen. The children carry their mother's last name, Padilla. The hammock is for the baby, who is about six months old. Nine year old Lionel shares a bed with his five or six year old sister and toddler brother. The toddler wears only a shirt, because he would soil pants. Toilet training doesn't seem to be an issue. Their thirteen year old daughter, Julia, shares a bed with her mother. Eduardo has his own bed.

Eduardo invited me to come back after dinner for a dance. When I arrived, Eduardo was playing a record outside for a group of about fifteen young men. At about 7:15pm we followed him and the record player to his house. His wife, her parents, four children and another old man were waiting inside. The room was lit by two kerosene "candles". Eduardo set up the record player while the guys (all males between sixteen and about twenty-four and apparently unattached) gathered. A dozen came inside and another dozen hung around outside the door. After one song, a commotion arose outside – "*Las bailadoras*" (girls dancers) were coming. Five girls (two under fourteen, one fifteen year old and the other two eighteen) entered in single file. Each one was decked out in a clean, pale pink dress, lipstick and shoes. The three older girls also had a thick layer of rouge. One girl had earrings and a ring; another was carrying a small baby (I don't know if it is her child.) They were followed by three smaller girls and a six-year-old boy (apparently younger siblings). The term "*bailadora*" definitely labels a girl as available and carries a positive connotation. Eduardo is proud that his daughter is one of them. Only one couple participated in the first dance. From then on, there were always four or five couples on the floor. The girl with the baby was the only *bailadora* to ever sit out a dance. The dancing is entirely a two-step, embracing in a ballroom stance, except that the man's left hand and the girl's right are folded firmly against their chests. About eight different tunes were played. One was definitely the favorite, getting about a third of the total air time. Once Eduardo played it four times in a row. Only about ten men did any dancing; the rest stood around smoking, chewing gum, and occasionally spitting on the floor. The spectators did very little talking. The male school teacher dropped by for a little while, but did not dance. The crowd started thinning out about 8:15pm. By 9:00pm, the grandparents had retired to the other room and we were down to one girl (Julia), five teenage boys and me. Throughout the dance, Eduardo stood by the record player, and watched with a smile.

Monday, July 26

Don Lelo led the planning, starting at breakfast. He expounded on his plans for us today, for Jaquith's next visit, for a trip to the beach at Puerto Cortes on Sunday, for establishing a permanent *Comite de Honduras y Cornell*, for running the *comedor*, and the next six years of projects. The success of yesterday's visit has really fired up his enthusiasm.

This was a real heavy work day. With eight local men helping, we hauled sand and cement, started laying the *comedor* floor, built a wire fence around it to keep the animals and kids off the wet cement, and dug the hole for the school's latrines. We are adding a third stool for the teachers at their request. (Nobody else in town has wanted a latrine.) The girls worked on desks – Sue varnished most of the boys' porch by knocking the varnish can over.

Manuel DuBon introduced me to *guaro* when I took an afternoon break. All the sweltering work had me worn out and thirsty. Today Ed's teasing was accurate; I was literally attached to my shirt. So, around 2:00pm I walked over the village "bar". The DuBons are the richest family in town. Manuel's wife owns the house and has a counter in one room where she sells cokes and beer. Their house has whitewashed wood siding and a wood floor – the only non-dirt floor I've seen in town.

Manuel was in the bar this afternoon, and he chatted while I sipped my warm Coke. He is about forty and muscular. He works as a cowboy for Raul Fernandez (Lelo's millionaire friend and Juan's countryman). Until we arrived, his watch was the only time piece in town. (Surprisingly, everybody seems to be able to tell you the time to the nearest half-hour by looking up at the sky.) He also owns a good radio. He claims to own 40 *manzanas* of land (almost seventy acres). Twenty are planted in corn, next to his cousin Eduardo's field. The rest are for grazing. He currently owns thirty head of cattle and is somewhat of a capitalist. He confided that he lent two hundred *Lempira* to the town drunk for six months without interest in exchange for five cows as collateral. He is confident that the loan won't be paid, so he will be able to keep the cows for what amounts to only twenty dollars a head. He told me he doesn't have many children because he spent eleven years in the prison in Omoa for shooting a man to death when both of them were drunk. I commented that it must have taken a lot of beer for them to get that drunk.

"We weren't drinking beer. *Guaro* is much stronger and better."

I had never heard of *guaro*. So he explained that it is made locally from sugar cane. He pulled out a bottle of clear liquid and a juice glass from behind the counter.

"For you, a free drink."

Thanking him, I raised the glass and took a sip. It burned my throat but left a nice aftertaste like licorice.

Manuel was watching and shaking his head. "Not like that. Men drink like this...." He raised his hand to his mouth indicating a quick swig.

I emptied the glass in two swallows, all except for a couple of drops that sprayed out when I gasped. The impact was immediate. I was already feeling dizzy and Manuel was chuckling. When I told him it was time for me to go back to work, the chuckle turned to a laugh.

The sunlight was glaring more than ever before as I staggered back to our house. I made it to my cot unassisted. Juan came over to see if I had gotten sick again. I grinned back, "Not sick, just temporarily incapacitated." He was familiar with *guaro*. Depending on the source, it is usually 160 to 180 proof. That juice glass was the equivalent to chugging six or seven shots of scotch. I was useless for the rest of the afternoon, even skipping the recess soccer game.

Four hours of rest and a good dinner revived me. Surprisingly, I don't have a hangover. As the alcohol wore off, the itching came back. All the members have developed a rash around our waists, which is probably caused by multiple chiggers getting as far as our belt lines and then nibbling away. We have affectionately designated this affection "galloping Chinese rot" by the team. The treatment was anything that might stop the itching. Doug developed a more irritating itch in his crotch. The rest of the boys teased him about it being a case of the crabs, but it turned out to be a fungal infection which Melissa treated with gentian violet and Tinaderm.

We ended the day with a long and heated discussion on the primary goals of the project and how a group of students like us could be most effective. We debated. Which is more important, material construction or social work? Should Cornell teams work in the same town year after year? It led to nothing like a unanimous consensus. The best suggestion (in my opinion) was that a first year team should concentrate on material work, because this makes it easier for the town to accept them and leaves tangible evidence of the progress. A smaller second year team would then focus chiefly on acting as liaisons for the town and teach town leaders how to use the resources available in San Pedro, etc. Any material project in the second year would be similar to the school garden here, for which Cornell and project friends helped obtained the materials, tools and seeds, but all of the planning and labor were done by the local school teacher and schoolboys. We all did agree that the real goal is to have enabled the local people to continue to improve their community after we have gone.

Tuesday, July 27

Everyone slept well, except Melissa, who had picked up a fever (probably from overwork) and Ed, who was rained on all night by termites falling from a rafter over his cot. Since Ed has made a show of inspecting bugs and playing with them, he got no sympathy from the rest of us. Melissa is a different story. She remained sick in bed all day, and we are all worried about her. Charlie brought Dr. Moreno over; luckily it is the Alliance Doctor's day in Quimistan. He thinks that it is a common parasite and gave her some pills. Juan, as usual, also thinks he is getting sick and got examined. Much to his dismay, his temperature is normal. He is just worn out. Juan has borne the brunt of the effort to draft a constitution for a committee to run the *comedor* that satisfies the various factions in town.

Charlie came today to make another latrine top with the help of Antonio. The boys continued with the floor of the comedor and the girls worked on desks. The school is looking good. In addition to the vegetable garden, the teachers have supervised the children's installation of flower boxes attached to the front windows.

We fixed and ate three meals.

This afternoon's visit from Don Pedro turned into a discussion of politics. He had heard on the radio that some groups of workers in Tegucigalpa had declared a strike and that many people demonstrated, showing a little restlessness. Pedro has been carrying his firearm, a Smith & Wesson .22 caliber revolver. He is ready to shoot it. He told us that the Liberals are bad people and he knows which people are Liberals and which are Nationalists. One of the main reasons that he has no sympathy for the Liberals is that he knows they have communist tendencies and that "Communism denies God and destroys the individual man." Also he wanted us to know: "There have previously been times of greater uncertainty and unrest than now, but when a Nationalist is in power, everything will be fine."

The main event of the day was a town meeting held to adopt the official organization for the *Comedor* committee, including electing the officers. The turnout was smaller than our previous meetings, but we still had thirty-five very interested participants from the town. The election of officers went smoothly. Juan presented a prospective slate, which was the result of a number of discussions and negotiations over the past ten days. The meeting simply approved it in a vote.

The structure of the committee turned out to be very bureaucratic and hierarchical, but so are the structures of all of the organizations (government and church) which they have experienced. We spent a lot of time on unimportant details, and the discussions showed a great deal of mistrust of other people in general. The meeting produced a few minor amendments to the proposed draft. Probably the most important change was the committee's name. The leaders did not want it to be limited to feeding the children. They are now the Milparada Committee for Progress. As always in Honduras, time was no factor, but even the natives began to get restless before the end. The meeting tried my patience, nevertheless, it is THEIR committee and we now have an official organization that meets the requirements CARE has for food distribution:

Constitution and Proposed Projects of the

"Comite Milparada Hacia el Progreso"

July 27, 1965

Milparada of Quimistan

Plan for the Committee of the *Comedor Infantil* Cornell

1. Composition of the Executive Commission:

President	Eduardo DuBon
Vice President	Laura de Machado
Voters: First	Juan Z. Hernandez
Second	Taurino Orellana
Third	Ma. Rosario Lopez
Fourth	Jose Orellana Torres
Fifth	Leonidas Pinto
Comptroller	Prof. Maria Luisa Perdomo
Treasurer	Antonio Machado
Vice-Treasurer	Lesby Gaido
Secretary	Pedro Hernandez
Vice-Secretary	Prof. Jacobo Munguia

2. Ex officio members

Sr. Abelardo Castillo, Mayor of the Municipality of Quimistan

Sr. Guillermo Rivera, Coordinator

Sr. Carlos Garcia, Coordinator

Sr. Desiderio Paz, Coordinator

Sr. Herberto Alcantara, District Supervisor of Schools

3. Commission in charge of storing the CARE food:

Juan Z. Hernandez	Depositor
Prof. Jacobo Munguia	Controller
Prof. Maria Luisa Perdomo	Controller
Ester Salvidar	Controller
Lesby Gaido	Controller

4. Scheduled meetings of the Executive Commission will need a quorum of seven members, four of these constituting a sufficient majority for making decisions.

5. In the absence of a quorum, a special meeting will be called for a later time. At this meeting, five will constitute a quorum and three will be a sufficient majority.

6. If it is not possible to summon a quorum, the meeting will be postponed until at least five members can meet.

7. The Executive Commission shall be elected yearly by the General Assembly, which consists of all of the members of the community.

8. The General Assembly, by a majority of one more than half, shall elect a new member in the case of resignation of a member of the Executive Commission because of health or other reason.

9. If a vote of the General Assembly fails to yield a majority, a new vote will be taken.

10. The General Assembly, that is the entire community, ought to contribute for possible expenses for maintaining the *"Comedor Infantil,"* such as trips to San Pedro Sula to obtain the supplies which CARE graciously provides whenever there is a responsible committee to operate the *comedor*.

11. The Executive Commission shall have the power to appoint, without the vote of the General Assembly, any necessary commissions, such as a commission in charge of maintaining the kitchen in working order, of bringing the food from San Pedro, etc.

12. As is characteristic of the democratic process, the General Assembly, that is the community, may ask that the Executive Commission meet to consider any matter of importance to the functioning of the *comedor* or the well being of the community.

13. The outgoing Executive Commission should, at the end of its term (one year), call a meeting of the General Assembly to elect a new Commission. Also, in this meeting, the Treasurer and the Comptroller should give a financial report. Also, the outgoing

Commission should, at this time, present or summarize the plans that they have carried out during their term and the plans for the future which for various reasons they have not been able to put into effect before this date.

The meeting also worked out a number of mechanical issues for the operating the *comedor*. A safe place was found to store the food. The Alliance Health Team volunteered to transport the supplies from San Pedro. Irma volunteered to cook with the other women helping her on a rotating basis. The children will wash their own dishes. I don't really know Irma, but the townspeople eagerly accepted her offer. The committee decided to pay her ten Lempira ($5.00) a month, if and when it could raise the money.

The new Executive Commission also made a list of other projects they want to undertake:

1. Finish the latrines for the school.
2. Construct a serving table for the kitchen of the *comedor*.
3. Construct a washstand, with an additional water tap near the *comedor* for washing dishes.
4. Construct a shower near the school.
5. Fence the school and comedor (if it is possible to get wire).
6. Plaster the outside of the school, and construct a cement patio in front of it.
7. Obtain books and build bookstands for a school library.
8. A program of latrine construction – with the assistance of the Alliance for Progress Mobile Health Team.

(They specified that the bigger projects, like numbers 4 and 6, should be scheduled for the dry season, when the townspeople have more free time.)

It was a long, arduous evening, but an important step forward.

Wednesday, July 28

We were all over the place today. Juan and Ed left early for San Pedro. Don Lelo went to Pinalejo and Quimistan. Trinchi, Sue and I went to Chiquila with Charlie of the Alliance and a load of wooden parts for CARE desks. Melissa was still recovering. That left Mary to hold clinic and Doug to work with two helpers on the *comedor*.

Chiquila is about thirty kilometers of bumpy road away. The people there are anxious for a Cornell team and it appears to be an excellent site. It is just off the highway from San Pedro to Santa Rosa de Copan, so there are good bus connections to San Pedro (a two-and-a-half hour trip). Also, the town of Sula, with a population of over a thousand, is just an hour's walk away. (That town has an Alliance clinic with a full time nurse and a weekly visit by the same doctor that serves Quimistan.) Chiquila is close to being a twin of Milparada, with a population of about four hundred and nothing else. Charlie ran a latrine program and about eighty percent of the houses participated. The only water supply is a river along the edge of town (so the team would need to use the Lister bags). The river is deep enough for bathing and runs dependably all year. The village is in desperate need of a new school. The current one is a mud structure about the size of the boys' house in Milparada. Fifty students sit and write on the floor. The materials we brought will let them build twenty-five desks, each seating two students. Looking at the school, I doubt that all of them will fit in the building. The community has land for the new building and offered to build the bricks (from mud and cement) before the team arrives. They want to convert the old school into a *comedor*. The village also needs a nurse and literacy program. The nearby town of Sula wants sixty-five desks for their school. Obviously Charlie has been spreading the word of our doings as he makes his rounds. There is a functioning town committee which sent two letters to Milparada, one thanking us in advance for the wood for the desks and the other formally asking for a team for next year.

After touring the town, our crew coached the schoolteacher and four other men in how to assemble CARE desks. Things went well, except the drill bit didn't last long. (Sue was glad to see someone else break one.) Charlie showed them how to make a new one from a nail and work proceeded. When we left at 3:00pm, they had two completed desks and the necessary tools to continue.

The trip back brought a nice surprise. Who should we see between Quimistan and home but "Melissa's" baby with both his parents. We stopped to admire the healthy boy.

Tonight's class attendance is down to ten, but all of them have obviously been studying the lessons between times. Melissa is back on the giving side of the medical ledger this evening.

Pressure is mounting on two fronts. We are running short on both time and money. I seem to be the only one worried about the latter. With only fourteen working days left, the materials for columns, roof and tables haven't arrived. Maybe tomorrow . .

We were ending the day as usual, gathered around our table when the radio brought stunning news from the outside world. On Radio Havana, Castro was in the middle of one of his harangues when we heard him say that "President Johnson is sending more than one hundred thousand soldiers to invade Vietnam in an attempt to crush the freedom loving revolutionaries under Ho Chi Min. This proves that the United States is still an imperialist nation trying to take over the whole world." Our first reaction was that Castro had gone overboard with his propaganda. This statement was absurdly unbelievable.

Doug switched the radio to the BBC. The calm reporter dryly confirmed the essence of the news. "During a noontime press conference, President Johnson announced he will send forty-four combat battalions to Vietnam increasing the U.S. military presence to one hundred twenty-five thousand men. To fulfill this commitment, thirty-five thousand men will be drafted into the army each month."

We did not get enough information to explain why this escalation was taking place. If anyone asks me why the gringos are doing this, I'll have to honestly tell them that I don't know. It just doesn't make sense. The closing comment about the draft puts a dark cloud over our futures. Yesterday, Pedro was expressing worries about unrest and uncertainty. Tonight we are going to bed with equally disturbing worries.

Thursday, July 29

Juan and Ed went to San Pedro yesterday in an attempt to expedite the arrival of the rest of the materials we need to finish our construction. They arrived in time to have breakfast and a haircut at the Hotel Bolivar before meeting with Beverly Kipps, the president of the Rotary Club and manager of the *Tobacalero Hondureno* (the national cigarette manufacturer). Kipps seemed to be very uninformed about our work. (He has just come back from a trip to England, so there is some excuse for his non-involvement.) They later met with Rafael Davila who invited them to attend that night's Rotary meeting. They then met Jaquith and Mr. Hayword, and did the necessary shopping. An encounter with Jacobo Laroche resulted in a donation of some more notebooks for the school.

Before the meeting, they met with Arnulfo who explained that the reason for our difficulties in getting the materials to finish the *comedor* was the result of internal difficulties in the club. Dr. Bendano spoke in very vague terms about "one more week." Paul Jaquith gave a wonderful presentation, followed by Rafael. Juan was asked to speak, and he decided to ask Armando (who had originally been skeptical about the project) to share his impression of the recent visit to Milparada. He spoke very well and is now clearly on our side. Still, they came back from San Pedro discouraged and without any firm commitments.

The rest of us basically just did our routine chores and waited for their return.

Marcos showed up early this afternoon. He brought me a fresh mango. It was about the size of a large apple with the texture of an overripe peach, but a better taste than either.

"Where did the mango come from?" I asked.

"A tree." Marcos replied with a grin.

"Whose tree?"

"Nobody owns the trees. They grow by the road and anyone can have any mango they pick."

I thought that was a marvelous idea and was ready to ask him to show me the trees so I could pick one for myself. But by then several other boys were around, a couple of them munching on their own mangos. When they heard that I liked the mango, several of them went running off to the north. Soon they were back with more than enough for the whole team. Marcos told me that I should eat just one a day. I figured that was a local rule to allow everybody to have a fair share. I didn't pass on that admonition when the other kids presented mangos to our girls.

We all enjoyed the tasty fruit. Several team members ate two or three. It turns out that the reason you should eat just one a day is that the fruit acts like a laxative. The people who enjoyed more than one paid the price by having bad cases of the runs by dinnertime. As Melissa noted: Diarrhea was combated with Nexoform, Kaopectate, or a powder preparation called Leoddahl.

Hayword is the Methodist chaplain at Cornell. He is newly appointed as the coordinator for the Cornell-in-Central America project. In my limited prior contacts with him on campus, he struck me as a mild-mannered, conservative dud.

Tonight we discussed the project with Jaquith and Hayword. It was an opportunity for us to try to explain to them what was wrong and what we thought about the future. Both of them tried to encourage us. They seemed to be genuinely pleased with how we are doing. All of the people they talked to in San Pedro gave favorable reports and it is obvious to them that we have established a good rapport with the villagers. That was enough to declare success. Six months ago, we might have agreed with them, but now we have developed a very different perspective. We told them that this project should accomplish more than a mystic or spiritual exchange of mutual understanding. Of course, that is valuable, but it comes naturally as a side effect of working together. We definitely feel an obligation to accomplish something that is more permanent and tangible. In some way, we must break the yoke of tradition, teach them to look ahead and make them want to help themselves. Without this, our stay would be a form of imposition which simply tantalizes them by showing them how poor their life is in contrast to ours.

The people who have really worked to help the villagers are Nelly, Don Lelo, Rafael, Charlie, and Guillermo. Only one of them is a member of the Rotary. We think that an independent committee of interested Hondurans would be more realistic and helpful, as a direct contrast with the Rotary Club. At the same time, we will continue to try to cultivate the Rotarians interest as a supplementary aid to us. Since they are the men of wealth and position in this country, they should be using their resources to help conditions in the villages. Hayword was receptive to the idea of having an additional group composed of the people who are actually doing the most to help our work. Some of us will go back to San Pedro to meet with key supporters to see if such a committee is practical.

We also reached agreement on recommending that a smaller, more specialized team would be most useful in a second-year situation and that a small village, such as Milparada is the best site, for a variety reasons that have become obvious to us. I'm not the only one who was disappointed by our visits to the prior sites in more-developed towns. A specific, academically-oriented report was also agreed to be advantageous from the point of view of obtaining money from foundations and generally broadening the understanding of what we do. We talked long into the night, covering possible plans for next year and the more specific plans for the next committee meeting. I was pleasantly surprised by Hayword – he really listened and wants to learn from us.

July 30 – 31

Mr. Hayword accepted Eduardo's invitation for a tour of his fields. Juan and I went with them right after breakfast. (Jaquith slept in.)

Hayword was naively enthusiastic about how green everything is. The DuBons have good bottom land, next to the road just across the river. Eduardo and Juan answered all of Hayword's questions, educating me about the agricultural practices in the process.

Corn and beans are the basis of the agriculture of the immediate region. Corn is planted from the fifth of July on and is harvested in August and September. A second crop is planted in October and November for harvest in February and March. (The dry season runs from late February into May). Farmers with level ground plow their field with a wooden plow pulled by oxen. The wood plows limit plowing to right after rain, so ground is soft enough. (Juan noted on the side that their plows are very primitive, similar to those used in ancient Egypt with the minor improvement of adding a steel tip.) The poorer families with hillside plots (like Marcos'), do all their "plowing" and weeding with a machete. The corn is allowed to grow for exactly twenty-two days before weeding begins. When in flower, the farmer bends each plant slightly so that the prevalent heavy rains will not damage the pollen.

Most of the harvested corn is immediately husked by hand and the grain is sold by weight. At the time of harvest, merchants from both Honduras and El Salvador visit the area to buy corn. The Banco Nacional de Fomento (BNF) is the biggest purchaser and has storage bins in Quimistan. Late in the dry season until the mid-August harvest, the stored corn sells for double the price the bank buys it for at harvest time.

The main consumption of corn is for tortillas. The lady of the house grinds the corn into a coarse meal, mixed with a little lime and water and cooks them on the stove top grill. Additionally some of the grain is used to fatten pigs for market.

Black beans are planted in May and September and are harvested in December and January. When the beans are two weeks old, it is time to clean out the weeds. The mature bean plants are pulled from the ground and hung in places sheltered from the rain until thoroughly dried before winnowing. Most of the beans are consumed by the family, but they can usually sell some to buy clothes. On the hillside fields (*milpas*), a*yotes* (gourds) are planted amongst the corn and beans. These are used for feeding livestock, and the dried gourds are also used as bottles and canteens, but the main reason for planting them is that the mixture keeps the land productive longer than if they just planted corn and beans.

Nearby (about twelve kilometers away, in the hills) coffee and cocoa are planted along with some potatoes. It takes five years after planting for coffee bushes to become productive, but then they have a long life (reputedly up to one hundred years) with the beans harvested once a year. Currently the raw beans are all trucked to San Pedro Sula for processing. (Don Lelo's wealthy friend is building a local coffee processing plant in Pinalejo.)

We saw some very healthy and good looking beef cattle pasturing in the fields near Milparada. As is usual in Latin America, they are a mixture of nearly every British- type cattle with some of the more recently introduced Brahma and Zebu breeds. I would venture to say that the cattle of the region are the best I have seen in Central America and in comparison to the cattle of Uganda and other parts of Africa, these animals look very well. I believe that one of the reasons for this phenomenon is the existence of very good pastures with many varieties of grasses. The United Fruit Company introduced Pangola and Parra grass to the region – both proven grasses in the tropical ecosystem and believed to be native to Africa. Parra grass thrives best in regions with a very heavy wet season and areas that are flooded during certain times of the year. Guinea grass is still the most popular pasture grass, mixed with Jaragua grass (introduced from Brazil). The beef cattle are mostly sold to Mexican and Guatemalan merchants for export.

There are also a number of milk producing cows in the vicinity, again of mixed origin. A great incentive has been created for this industry by the establishment of a modern dairy processing plant in San Pedro Sula, "*Leche Sula*". It buys the milk at the farms along the Pinalejo - Quimistan road using modern tank trucks to ship it to San Pedro. All of the milking is done by hand, as is usual in the tropics. The sanitary standards of *Leche Sula* are undoubtedly equal to the most stringent regulations of the dairy industry in New York State. The plant packages pasteurized milk in modern tetra-packs and also produces cheese, butter and ice cream. According to some of the local informants, the largest number of cows found at a dairy farm is one hundred. Locally, any unsold milk is used for fattening pigs, rather than for human consumption.

While we were out, Ed had walked to Quimistan and contacted Don Lelo. He is arranging a meeting of interested people in San Pedro for tonight.

Just as Juan, Trinchi and I, plus Hayword, were planning to take off for Quimistan, a wide-eyed frightened looking young woman brought Juancito to our house. He was writhing in pain and holding his stomach. His breathing was coming in gasps. The sobbing mother told us that her other son had acted like this last year and died a couple of days later. Melissa examined him and diagnosed a possible appendix problem. We decided to take him with us to San Pedro for hospital treatment. This announcement did not get the expected response from the mother. "Hospitals are where people go to die." Since her knowledge is based on the quack's place in Quimistan, she is probably right. We explained that the hospital in San Pedro had good doctors and they could probably cure Juancito so he could live for a long time. All that Melissa could do for him was to give him some pills to numb the pain. In a desperate act of faith, she entrusted Juancito to my care. We were her only hope. I tried to hide my fear that his appendix might burst before we got him to a hospital and we would have a dead boy on our hands. The prospect of doing nothing was worse.

Juan went ahead to try to borrow a Jeep, while the rest of us walked. I carried Juancito most of the way. It seemed as if we were running out of luck. We were stuck in Quimistan for three hours, drinking Cokes and trying to flag down trucks. The bus had arrived late with two flat tires and no spare, so it wouldn't be going any farther today. Juancito was still in pain and scared to death. He kept whining, "*Queiro vivir*" ("I want to live.") and "*Me quiere ir a mi casa.*" ("I want to go home.") I did the best I could to calm him down, but I couldn't blame him. The waiting was pure agony.

By pure luck, the "*Amigos de Honduras*" truck came along and took us all to the city. Our first stop was the Bandanos' clinic – neither doctor was there, so we had to go on to the general charity hospital. There were soldiers at the doors, mostly keeping people out. Inside people were sitting and lying on floor – the place was filthy. Being gringos and knowing the director, we were waited on right away. The boy was X-rayed, which showed that his appendix was OK. He had a bad bronchial infection and was draining mucus into his stomach, but the real problem was the tapeworm had grown so large that it was starting to clog his digestive tract. They brought Juancito back to the reception area and gave him medicine for bronchitis, which soon had him breathing easier. If the tapeworm was left alone, he probably would not last through the next dry season. The doctor explained that they could kill the tape worm with a poison. Poisoning and extracting the tape worm would take a few hours and the patient would be very weak when the procedure was finished. He offered to keep him in the hospital overnight. Juancito was clinging to me and wouldn't speak at all. I asked if I could be in the room with him while they got rid of the worm. He said, "No, it will be messy and smelly. You would get sick and be in the way." We consulted among ourselves. We had come this far and Juancito would not have another chance to get treatment for the tapeworm. But as we looked around at the crowded mix of people with all kinds of infections and diseases, Juan observed that it appeared to be irresponsible and dangerous to leave him over night in a ward full of people with different diseases. I was also upset by the idea of leaving Juancito alone with strangers when he was in so much misery. So we agreed to having the procedure but said we would come back and pick him up after our meeting.

We went on to the Columbia Hotel for dinner and on to the Hotel Bolivar for the committee meeting. The initial meeting of the *Equipo do Honduras y Cornell* garnered Don Lelo, Nelly Duarte, Arnulfo Gutierrez, Charlie Garcia, Senora de Geul, Senora de Gutierrez (Arnulfo's wife) and the wife of the Chief of the Armed Forces, along with the four of us. A number of others had signed up for the committee but couldn't make this session on short notice. It was a small, but enthusiastic group of people who feel strongly about the value of the project and want to see it continue. Senora Guel brought some new ideas. It was felt that this should be a coordinating committee with an informal structure. The group agreed on a list of purposes and tasks for the committee:

1)   Help choose the locations, gather facts and make plans for work projects.

2)   Increase publicity in the newspapers (because no one in San Pedro knows enough about the project).

3)   Contact all the leading organizations in town, make them aware of us and establish connections so they can help us and we can possibly help their programs (CARE, Alliance, SCIDE, Bicultural General, etc).

4)   The committee would also have things prepared before the team arrived so no time will be lost in collecting materials (like this year).

5)   Somehow work with the university students of Honduras. As Senora Guel said, "They must be made aware, to recognize the problems of their country. Now, they don't understand. Students are the most effective means to cross the gap. They have energy, time and drive. This should be taken as an opportunity to work in the rural areas – to know their country."

6)   As a follow-up program, the committee can develop long-term aims that need not be interrupted for nine months, but can be checked up on while the Cornell students are gone.

In summary it was an optimistic and reassuring meeting. The committee will meet again in Milparada on August 15.

After the meeting we took a cab to pick up Juancito. The doctor said the procedure was successful. They had evacuated twenty-six feet of tapeworm from the boy. It is surprising that he had lived this long. Juancito was pale and trembling slightly. He still wouldn't say a word. We went on to Swanson's and got to our guest rooms at 10:30pm. Juancito shared a room with a double bed with me. He reeked. The odor was a combination of old dirty sweat, putrid smells from the hospital, and stale urine. I tried to get him to take a bath and let me wash his clothes. He shrank back from the tiled bathroom – maybe it looks too much like the operating room. He wouldn't take off his clothes or let go of my arm. We were all exhausted, so I gave in, took off my shoes, socks and shirt and got into bed. It still took awhile to get the kid calmed down and lying on his own side of the bed, so I could roll on my side and breathe clean air. I'm not sure how long it took to drift off to sleep.

He woke me up about 1:00 am with a loud cry. I asked what was wrong. "Bad dreams." He was having nightmares. I tried to calm him down with quiet talk and singing a lullaby, but he wouldn't settle down or stop crying. I finally moved over and put my arm around his shoulder. His body was stiff with tension, but he snuggled up against me and quieted down. After another lullaby, his body relaxed and he went to sleep. I was not in a comfortable position and his aroma added to my discomfort. I never got back to sleep. I felt helpless today, but what else could I do?

We got up at 7:30 and ate breakfast with Mr. Swanson. He is a self-confident, energetic young executive-type. He is a very nice guy and greeted Juancito kindly. After eating, we read newspapers and the kid went back to sleep. Nelly came by at about 10:00am to pick us up. Juancito was feeling better and enjoyed the trip back, smiling most of the way. He remained very subdued and hadn't recovered his usual energetic jumpiness. He spoke only to me and only a few words. We stopped by Nelly's place in Cofradia so she could load us up with more gifts of fresh food.

Juancito's mother was overcome by joy at his return. She expected that she would never see him again. The reunion brought tears to my eyes and made last night's discomfort seem like nothing.

There wasn't much work done in our absence. The supplies still hadn't arrived. The remaining team members had just done some general clean up, and saw some patients and took an afternoon siesta.

Our lab technician friend from Quimistan came over after dinner. He just "stopped by to say hello" and to tell us we hadn't kept faith with him regarding the woman we took to San Pedro instead of entrusting her to his willing hands.

Nelly is spending an amazing amount of time helping us. She stayed over with us tonight. Tomorrow, she will be driving the team to a day at the beach.

Sunday, August 1

We went to bed last night with visions of a day at the beach in Puerto Cortez dancing in our heads. The girls were soon awakened by a clatter at their back door. Nelly sprang from her bed to see what was the matter. A cow had gotten into the yard and was eating our bar of soap and a sponge.

We were awake relatively early this morning in an attempt to start our trip to Puerto Cortes at a decent hour. Pedro and Antonio came to the house about 7:00am to join us. While standing out front waiting for us to finish up the dishes, the two became engaged in a rather violent argument with the owner of the boys' house. The general theme of the discussion seemed to concern the injustice we were doing this man by not equipping his house with water facilities. He felt slighted because we have installed two water taps in the girl's house and none is his. The home owner accused Antonio of using his influence against him. The truth is that it was Juan's decision, backed by the rest of the boys, to share the water tap at the girl's house instead of spending more time on ourselves. Pedro kept quiet. Antonio tried to explain to him that whatever the team had done was for the interest and benefit of the community and the younger generation, and that it was wrong to be only interested in his own house. The man then accused Antonio of receiving money from the Cornell group and stomped away. This left Antonio feeling very discouraged. He told us this man is "round like a ball" (I guess that means slippery) and that we cannot help him or change his attitude.

We climbed into Nelly's pickup (four in the front and six in the back) and started out for the beach at 8:00am. We turned around at 8:01 to shut the door of the Boys' house. When we stopped at Nelly's house in Cofradia to pick up food and Chito, we were mobbed by a fantastic assortment of animals - hens, guinea fowl, geese, ducks, dogs, turkeys and more – all wanting attention and/or food. We continued on to San Pedro, where we again stopped for gasoline, bread and ice. About 10:00am we were leaving San Pedro, traveling on a paved road for the rest of the way to Puerto Cortes. Puerto Cortes is the best port in Honduras and the main shipping point for bananas. One hour later, the blue waters of the Atlantic Ocean were before us – a beautiful sight for dust-ridden eyes. I was expecting a busier site. The bay is rather small, with a narrow sandy beach with coconut palms. We had about fifteen feet of bright white sand between the palm trees and the surf.

We drove to the house of a friend of Nelly's. The house is located among the coconut palms on sandy soil. It is an extremely modern structure, built up on stilts, so the living quarters wouldn't be harmed by hurricane tides. This is the Canahuates' beach house. It has a spacious yard and luxurious living quarters on the second floor with a porch in the shade underneath. Behind the main house they have a huge TV antenna tower (they can pick up broadcasts from Miami) and a good-looking wooden house where the servants live. The Canahuates are the richest family on the North Coast and also have homes in San Pedro and Miami and an apartment in Paris.

We swam in the clear water directly in front of the house. The beach drops off slowly; I could still stand touching the bottom up to five hundred feet out. The waves were gentle, only about a foot tall. We all enjoyed the warm water, even though it was extremely salty. I spent a little time looking for sea shell and only found a few snails. We could see a wrecked ship stuck in the sand further down the beach. It had been left by Cuban refugees. It looked like it had never been seaworthy.

The ensuing lunch was unbelievable, undoubtedly the best meal we have eaten in Honduras. After an obvious display of gluttony, we took a half-hour siesta under the palm trees in the front yard. During lunch, our hostess explained that her family are Arab Christians. They were merchants who had to flee the Ottoman Empire to avoid persecution. The Arab Christians lost everything they owned and had to start from nothing when they settled in Central America. "The governments here are not stable, so we must be ready to flee again in the event of a revolution or dictator. That's why we keep our money in banks in the United States and Switzerland. It is not safe to invest in Honduras. Also, we have to go to Miami to get good medical care and send our children away to go to school in the United States or Europe."

I am uncomfortable with her smugness and lack of concern for the poor conditions for most of her countrymen. She is chain smoking imported cigarettes while she explains that her family's wealth is the result of their hard work and intelligence. "The *mestizos* work hard with their bodies but aren't intelligent enough to run a good business. We take good care of our servants and they appreciate us and take good care of us." Her tone is patronizing and I want to argue with her. The people of Milparada are not short of intelligence, they only lack education and opportunities. As I tried to frame my argument, I realized that I had been raised with the same family belief that if you got an education and worked hard, like my immigrant grandparents did, you would succeed in life. The United States is the land of opportunity, but now I have to wonder if the migrant farm workers and the Blacks in the inner city slums really could escape poverty if only they worked hard.

It was decided that we would take a trip to Omoa, site of a prior Cornell team in the North Coast region. The road forded three rivers before rising to a hilltop that provided a beautiful view of the entire bay and beyond.

We passed through banana plantations owned by the United Fruit Company. From our readings, I thought of United Fruit as a villain. It has a reputation for exploiting Central Americans and interfering with their government through threats and bribery. Still, these plantations looked prosperous and the field hands have a better standard of living than the average farmer or laborer. The official work day for field workers is 6:00-11:00 am then 12:00-4:00pm with a daily wage of three Lempira ($1.50). That used to sound ungodly low, but it is triple what the lumber company pays Marcos' brother. The company maintains a free health service and schools – the buildings look modern and clean. Employees can rent low-cost housing for their families. These are small wooden cabins; still high quality compared to the housing in Milparada. The social concern is that if an employee quits or is fired, his family is evicted and loses the medical and education benefits.

It was only a half-hour drive to Omoa. Omoa is a nice looking small town. The house the Cornell team stayed in is a painted wood structure with flowers planted in front. It would look like a small working class home in the United States, except it is painted a bright shade of blue.

The special attraction in Omoa turned out to be an old Spanish fort that had later been converted into a prison -- a most interesting structure. The Castillo de San Fernando has such a thick wall that the inside perimeter is 519 feet and the outside is 634 feet around. It was built by Spaniards in the 1770's and served as a prison from 1820 into the 1950's. Now it is a National Monument. There was a guard/guide at the entrance, but once inside, we were free to roam around. It is double walled. The outer wall is a ten foot high stone defensive position. There are a large number of old cannons and cannon balls lying around, rusting away. The inner wall is twenty feet high and about feet thick containing twenty foot long windowless vaults that served as the prison cells. It is famous for ex-torture chamber. The primary form of torture was dripping boiling water on the victim's head. If he survived twenty-four hours without confessing, he would be set free. Most died after seven about hours. Pedro was unusually quiet and pensive as we walked around. Finally he said that his father had been a prisoner here for ten years. (That explains the eleven year gap in ages between Pedro and his younger brother.)

The return trip was relatively unexciting. We got a royal greeting at Milparada, especially Marcos, both Nicos and Roberto (who had a cut on his head for Melissa to treat). The boys wanted to hear all about what we saw and did.

We got back just in time to fix a late dinner and go to bed.

Monday, August 2

We dragged ourselves out of bed sevenish and downed the usual oatmeal mush for breakfast. Trinchi just couldn't make it this morning; she just smiled, rolled over and went back to sleep.

Sue mangled her fourth drill bit. She was upset because the salt water had left her hair kinky (even after last night's shower). Since we couldn't work on the comedor, she got far more attention and help in redoing her hair than she wanted.

La Professora Maria Luisa was ill and couldn't teach, so I became the volunteer substitute for the third graders. The kids started giggling as soon as I started writing on the board. It took a little while to find out why. It turns out that writing with your left hand is not permitted. "You are supposed to only use your right hand. I tell them that for me, the left hand is the right one to use. (That pun is one of the few that actually translate.) I substituted an English lesson for the morning reading, so that went reasonably well.

The mathematics lesson was mostly subtraction. Disaster struck when I worked the first problem on the board as an example. The problems involved four-digit numbers. The first step involved borrowing and as soon as I crossed out the tens digit and reduced it by one, the kids looked confused. I tried to explain why it worked, but the kids were saying "No. No, that is wrong." Finally Victor came out to show me the correct way to do the problem. They have been taught to subtract the top digit from the larger bottom one and then figure out how much more it takes to make it one. Next they add one to the digit for the next place on the bottom. For example, for $46 - 17$, the first calculation is that taking 6 from 7 leaves one, so you need 9 more to make 10. The extra 10 changes the 1 to a 2 and 4 minus 2 is two, so the answer is 29. The concept of borrowing is alien to them. The embarrassing thing is that it took me so long to understand their method, which is equally logical. I also tripped up by writing a seven written without including a crossbar. The style is said to have originated with National Lottery printing them in a way that couldn't be altered to look like an eight or nine.

By the afternoon writing class, the moving around and talking was really getting on my nerves. It probably wasn't that much worse than what I had observed before, but I had been struggling to find the right words for explaining things and my patience was running out. Without a leather strap or cane in my hand, the boys saw no reason to obey my command to sit down and be quiet. Darnella Rivera became my favorite student, at least temporarily. She is quiet unless called upon, but an alert listener with a sharp mind. She had the only perfect paper on the writing assignment the day I gave. For Social Studies, I stuck to the book but tried to call on individual students so each one would have a turn. Also, I was not very good at picking out the correct answer and who said it from the chorus of voices. That was a frustrating and ultimately wasted effort. Their habits were too well ingrained.

Tonight I counted my remaining money and decided I had better simplify my plans for the return trip. I'll have to skip the side trip to Veracruz and the beach, and I'll take up Stuart's offer of a bed at his parent's place in Mexico City. I've just finished sending him a note and writing another letter home:

Mon. 8-2

Dear family

Things are kind of bogged down waiting for material, but there is still lots to do. I substituted for a sick teacher - what an experience!

I've reached the point of being slightly tired all the time, (plus my legs are covered with bites) but the only thing that bothers me is the thought of leaving when there's so much left to do.

We're moving around more - this Sunday a friend took us all to Puerto Cortez and Omoa (in the back of a pick up) for a swim in the ocean and sight-seeing. There's an old Spanish fortress at Omoa that was used as a prison until 1957. (We found out that the father of the richest man in Milparada spent 11 years there for murder).

One minor change in plans - I will go by Puebla and Oaxaca instead of Veracruz and will be staying in a private home in Mexico City instead of a hotel.

I tried a little guaro the other day - boy is that stuff strong, but the surprising part is that it tastes like licorice.

I'm getting quite accustomed to the life here. (Mom, you'd love it except for the dirt) and I'm afraid I'll have culture shock when I get back to the States. It's gotten so that a house looks ritzy if it has got a good coat of whitewash.

Good-bye for now, Dick

Materials for the *comedor*? The situation is getting quite worrisome. Unless the Rotary comes through, we will leave behind a foundation and a third of a slab floor. That would be a horrible repeat of their experience with having a half-finished school sitting on the edge of town for three years. Without a proper *comedor*, the town won't be eligible for CARE food. All of the efforts that the townsmen have put in helping us would be for naught. Somehow we will have to figure out a way to get it built.

Tuesday, August 3

Trinchi recovered.

I attempted to teach school again. Boy, will I be glad to get back to a less hopeless job.

The other boys helped haul firewood for the *comedor's* kitchen. In the process, Juan and Ed almost got run over by a pair of oxen in the greatest chase scene since the Keystone Kops. A couple of townsmen finished digging the latrine hole – six feet deep, it looked just the right size for a grave. Mary played washer woman and Sue spent the whole day working on desks without damaging anything.

Juan entertained the town in the afternoon by wandering around in his swim suit and taking a shower in daylight. Ed, Doug and Melissa walked to Quimistan and came back with bread, Starlac powdered milk and two copies of an "urgent" telegram from Don Lelo. (The third copy came by "pony express" a little later.) The telegram brought the good news that the materials will come in a couple of days.

Today's excitement came courtesy of one of the young farmers. He came back from the fields with a six-and-a-half foot long boa constrictor he had killed. It was a great find for him. He can sell it to a man in Quimistan who makes fancy belts. Some of the innards will be used for "medicine." The ten Lempira ($5.00) the skin will fetch is almost two weeks' income.

Speaking of creatures, I'll catalog the animal life we have encountered along with the school boys' opinions of them:

- Snakes – The velvet snakes (*venadores*) we've killed are the most dangerous ones. There are more types and bigger ones in the mountains. Different boys give vastly different opinions on how common they are.
- Opossum – I saw one that one of the boys killed with his sling shot. They aren't good to eat. He killed it because "it eats chickens."
- Iguana – I've seen lots of them out of the windows when we are on the road, but very few near towns. That's because they are considered a delicacy, so the boys actively hunt them with there slingshots.
- Rabbits – There are lots in the mountains and they are considered good food. They are seldom hunted by the boys because they are hard to hit with a slingshot. The men who have guns shoot them regularly.
- Rats – Rats are common in San Pedro Sula and along the coast, but there aren't many around Milparada. They are almost impossible to

keep out of the house. The boys view rats as a danger to their food supply, especially as eaters of stored corn. They don't consider them a health hazard.

- *Sapos* (Toads) – There are lots and lots. They are noisy at night. One type, called *Boujo* based on the sound it makes, is particularly active and loud after a heavy rain. You should not touch one because it secretes a white "milk" from it pores which is supposedly very bad for people.
- *Loros* (Parrots) – Parrots are only found in the mountain forests, but they are abundant there.
- *Sopelotes* - These are scavenger birds. (It is also the name for a potent mixed drink.) They are all around. They are viewed a garbage collectors. They are good because they clean up dead things. They are also protect by law. There is a one hundred Lempira ($50) fine for killing one.
- *Gaballina* – This is a pretty, bright orange chicken hawk. The locals consider it a bad bird, for the obvious reason.
- Tarantulas – They're around in large numbers. The younger boys hunt them by dropping a bean on a string into holes. The spider bites the bean and the boy pulls him up and kills him. They don't think tarantulas bother people, but they are very bad for horses and cattle because they bite around the base of a leg and their venom ends up destroying the hoof
- *Grillo Cantador* – This is a strange looking arachnid. Its body is flat, mud-grey about one-and-a-half inches long with three pairs of functional long thin legs and a front pair of hooked appendages which are covered with barbs. These front legs are usually folded tight against its head, so they look almost like huge compound eyes. It also has a pair of long hair-thin S-shaped feelers. It is supposed to be common, but I have only seen one.
- Lizards – Honduras is home to many varieties of lizards. Some are very colorful.
- Scorpions – The roofs of houses seem to be the favored habitat for scorpions. The local variety is mud-grey, not deadly nor feared. Nico was stung by one while we were gone in Teguligalpa. The effect of the sting is to make your heart beat fast. Nico didn't mind getting stung because the cure is to eat lots of sweets.
- Wild honey bees – The bees are all black and smaller than ones we are used to in the United States.
- Honey Wasps – These are small, stingless insects. Their honey is a real treat.
- Wingless wasps – On the other hand the wasps that live in *cachilla* thorns are vicious and feared. They bother both people and cattle.

- Mosquitoes – There are very few mosquitoes in town, but swarms of them in the hills. They are known to drink blood and cause fevers.
- *Cucarachas* – Cockroaches are one the of few bugs that are viewed as pests. They should be killed whenever you see one.
- *Mariposas* (butterflies) – I was expecting to see some exotic butterflies in the tropics. Instead, I have just seen lots of small yellow and white ones.
- Moths – Just like everywhere else, they come in swarms to our kerosene lantern, or any other source of bright light in the evening.
- River Shrimp – These grow to nine or ten inches long in the larger, slow flowing rivers. There are none around here.

Moscarones – This is the generic name for mostly harmless bugs of a variety of types. This category includes:

- Fireflies can be seen by the thousands shortly after dusk.
- Beetles come in a wide variety of shapes and sizes. Some are over two inches long.
- Wood ants are common and up to an inch long. They don't bite.
- Corn-leaf-eating ants do have stinging bites. I saw one ant hill that was six feet in diameter.
- Fleas and chiggers are hard to see. Their bites are the cause of our "galloping Chinese rot" rash. They don't seem to bother the natives.
- Termites are all over the place. The people know that they eat wood. They are the main reason houses have to be rebuilt after ten to twelve years. But they don't worry about them or try to kill them, probably because they are so common that eradicating them would be a hopeless task.
- Flies apparent start breeding when the rain comes. There were very few when we arrived, but they have gotten progressively worse.

The evening discussion was mostly devoted to figuring out how to avoid doing nothing until the supplies come. We should only have to kill a couple of days more, if the Rotary Club comes through.

Wednesday, August 4

We witnessed a bullfight today. It was not the planned kind with a matador, but it did bring some excitement into our routine. For some reason, a pair of bulls had wandered on to the plaza. The fight amounted to a test of strength between the two, with one trying to use his horns to hurt the other. After quite a while, the collisions and thrusting came to a rather uneventful end. The larger bull, which had shorter horns, just sort of walked away leaving the field to the smaller animal. Moral: "He who perseveres, though he may be weaker, will win the battle."

The last desk, number fifteen, was finished today – the wood was so badly warped that it needed a few alterations with a saw. After the initial confusion of a variety of opinions on just what was the best method for assembling the desks, the project settled down and went smoothly. Each completed desk was given two coats of varnish for protection. To best utilize our time and available tools, one person would assemble desks while another varnished.

Sue has definitely taken the lead, not only in the construction but in touting the project. I recorded her evaluation:

> The desks were a good project for the girls. The Hondurans saw us doing physical work which was not part of their concept of a woman's role. They gradually accepted it and began to realize that the girls as well as the boys wanted to get out and work hard to accomplish something. Often village men offered their help, either out of courtesy of genuine interest; and although they usually botched the job, it was an important step in the direction of cooperation and understanding our intentions. It was also a more tangible result with a more immediately obvious practicality than our larger project, the *comedor*, the purposes of which were more long range and complex. From our point of view, the desk project was also purposeful. It provided a tangible feeling of accomplishment for the girls who otherwise would be totally occupied with the more frustrating and remote tasks of teaching and housework.

I still attract a knot of boys every afternoon. Now they are the ones asking questions, mostly wanting to hear about things in the United States. I'm having a hard time with some of the answers. It is not so much a problem of language as a problem in finding appropriate comparisons. How do you describe New York City and its subways to a group of people who have never seen a train track or a building taller than two stories? Some of my tales must seem as fantastic to them as the genies and flying carpets of the Arabian Nights. I can't imagine explaining what Disneyland is like to these boys. I try to give a balanced view of our country. After describing my parents' house, I pointed out that the most of the people who work in the fields, weeding and harvesting crops, live in houses that are not much different than the wooden ones on the banana plantations here.

Our kerosene lantern died. We've added mantels to the shopping list for the next trip into San Pedro. By the way, the food was very good today. Also, Doug finished our letter to the U.S. Ambassador.

It seems that many of the prominent men in town are busy going off to the coffee *fincas* in the hills. It is a way to earn cash while the corn is ripening. Attendance at our literacy and English classes is suffering the consequences.

We hope tomorrow brings Juan, Ed and Don Lelo with the material we need. It's hard to believe that our time here is almost up and we are all feeling anxious about finishing the *comedor*.

Thursday, August 5

Ed and Juan again went to San Pedro based on the telegrams and letters (seven of which arrived on Tuesday) from Don Lelo stating that the Rotary Club had decided to provide us with materials to complete our construction projects.

Another one of Don Lelo's connection solved the problem of getting for the materials. A man from nearby Pinalejo carries a load of lime into San Pedro daily, usually returning with an empty truck. Thus, he was persuaded to haul our building materials and other required items from San Pedro.

Most of our other chores are done on an "I feel like it" or an "I guess it ought to be done" basis. Today, laundry fell into the second category. Plus I had nothing else to do this morning. The social laundry area of the river is strictly women's territory. So when the boys do laundry it is a solo task using a washboard and laundry tub in the backyard. Even there, men doing laundry is cause for chuckles and teasing.

I went for a stroll during the after lunch siesta period. Juancito's mother saw me and asked me to come in and let her serve me lunch. The lunch was a tortilla and a cup of coffee. She was full of thanks for my "saving" Juancito. I tried to redirect the credit to the doctor, where it belongs. The main thing is that Juancito is now feeling better and can do more work than ever before.

Their house is one of the smallest stick houses in the village. It is a single room, about ten feet by fourteen feet with one door and one window. The furnishing is a single bed, a burlap bag hung up to be a hammock for the baby, a bench, a small table, a shelf along one wall and two boxes.

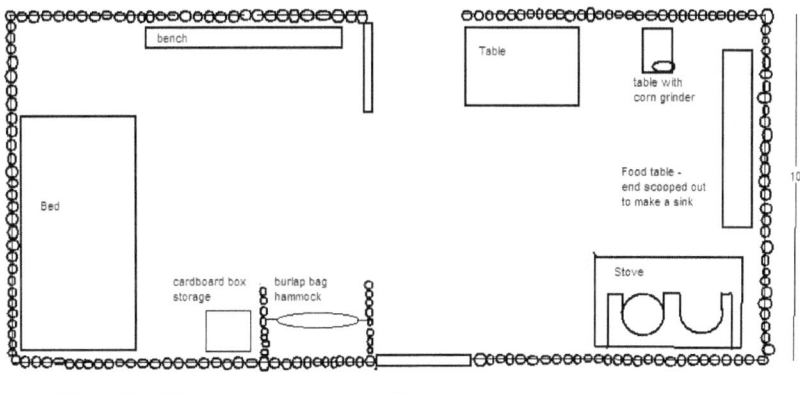

Figure 6. Juancito's house

Yesterday I wrote about the value of building desks. Tonight I'll give equal time to our literacy classes. The Honduran illiteracy rate is generally estimated as about sixty-five percent. Neighboring Nicaragua, with roughly as many schools, has a rate of fifty percent and Guatemala, with one-fifth the number of schools has a rate of seventy-two percent, only slightly higher than that of Honduras. This anomaly is undoubtedly explained in terms of the relative progressiveness of the political regimes in power and their emphasis on education. Part of our job this summer in Milparada is to expose the illiterates to their language in the form of oral exercises through the use of the *Alfalit* series of instruction books, published for that purpose by the Evangelical Association.

Interest in our language instruction by and large has been satisfying, but many of those who otherwise would have been reading often slipped over to the next room to audit the English classes. Eduardo is the only adult who attended regularly and conscientiously. I think he fully realized the necessity of being able to read and regretted having to work in the fields as a child, and thereby having received little or no schooling. His progress was gratifying and gave an aura of success to the program.

In addition to the *Alfalit* books, the CARE village library came in very handy for oral practice. There were a number of men and teens who could already read a little bit and who welcomed the opportunity to read aloud three times a week. As far as can be determined, there were no books in town other than one copy of each elementary text book, so practice was understandably slow and difficult at first. The pupils were encouraged to choose their own books from a selection of forty titles or so, then to read aloud at their own pace, each to his own teacher. They had been taught to read any Spanish word phonetically, but did not understand a lot of what they read. Asking a reader "What does that mean?" would often bring only a shrug or "I don't know" when an unusual word was encountered. Nevertheless, they did practice enthusiastically.

At first I had worried that the main draw was getting attention from us, especially when a teen was reading to one of our girls. That view was too cynical. They really wanted to read and find out more about the world. When Trinchi first moved Nicolas Cruz out of the *Alfalit* pamphlets, they began by reading a book on the continents of the world, stopping when he became tired. What a joy when he asked her to lend him the book and two others as well! Then his friends asked for the same. We've lent out some dozen books from the CARE library between each class session.

Many of the books were returned; a few were not. It doesn't really matter. They will stay in town and be read and reread till their covers are worn off. One of the top projects the Comedor Committee wants to undertake is to build book shelves in the school and get more books. The people know they are poor and recognize their illiteracy, but as long as they keep asking for books and retain the desire to learn and improve themselves, there is hope for the future. The literacy classes have been the most gratifying part of our work in Milparada so far.

Friday, August 6

Yesterday Juan and Ed spent most of the day going from sawmill to sawmill in the rain to find suitable wood. There were a number of delays and some people were skeptical about the Rotary Club and its ability to pay the bills. Everyone thinks highly of them, but for various reasons the club seems to be in a precarious financial situation. By evening, they had purchased the wood, cement and asbestos roofing along with nails, bolts and other necessary hardware.

Ed took a cab bright and early to see Fermin Aplicano's place. The older gentleman was the first choice because he is a close friend of Don Lelo. But of course, he wasn't in. So Ed proceeded to Charlie Daniel's sawmill. Charlie wasn't in either, but his accountant, Carlos, was and assured Ed, "Yes the order is ready; we are just waiting for a truck." So he waited five hours, during which time a Honduran Indian employee of the mill took him to his home to admire his hibiscus collection and have lunch. Once they got the truck loaded, the driver determined that the load was too heavy to take on the cement and roofing as well.

When they stopped by to leave the invoices with Arnulfo, the young secretary engaged him in conversation. She had gone to school in New Orleans for a few months but didn't like it so she came back home. "And anyhow, how CAN you stand those filthy Indians in Maili... what's its name? Haven't you all gotten sick? Don't forget you simply must have an exit visa before leaving Honduras."

Ed and Juan said good-bye to San Pedro, with its hot sidewalks, beggars and street urchins, petty bureaucrats, hawkers on the street corners and eager taxi drivers. By now even Ed speaks of Milparada as "home".

They got home around 8:00 pm and we all helped unload the wood.

Tomorrow, the truck should make a return trip with the roofing and cement. We will be gone. The sightseeing trip to the Mayan ruins in Copan was scheduled before we left the United States.

When we return, we will be ready for the final push. The *comedor* will get built. It WILL GET BUILT.

Saturday, August 7

We had a leisurely morning. We packed our small bags and walked to Quimistan to catch another one of our wonderful Honduran buses. Leaving Milparada at 9:30am, we arrived in Quimistan at10:30am and boarded the 11:00am bus at 11:50am. It was a twenty-four passenger school bus with forty people inside and one clinging to the luggage rack on top. Our companions included crying babies, rolling watermelons, spitting men and smelly animals, not to mention the dust from the bumpy road. This time we headed away from San Pedro to see the famous Mayan ruins at Copan.

We arrived at La Entrada, where the road branches off at 1:50pm. There sixteen people climbed on a large model Jeep – four on the front seat, eight in back, three on the running boards and one on the back bumper (holding on to the ladder). Compared to the sweltering school bus, riding on the running board, with one arm hooked through the window post, was a pleasant adventure. The road took us up into the mountains, and was paved with boulders and ruts. The driver had a sadistic sense of humor. He purposely drove over the top of a rooster and later a dog, catching neither with the wheels, so they both were able to run off as soon as we passed. After a couple of brief stops, where five of the other passengers got off, we arrived in Copan at 5:30pm (with everyone inside for the last hour). Copan is a picturesque town. The residents are heavy to Indian blood and some dressed like the National Geographic pictures of Guatemalan Indians. We are close to the border. Guatemalan Quetzal notes are as common here as Honduran Lempiras.

As we came into town, I noticed a number of houses adorned with Coca Cola ads and the words "Aqui me quedo" (Here I stay). The driver stated that those signs outside a house indicates love for sale.

There are two hotels in town. We are staying in Hotel Maya. It has electricity from a generator between 6:00pm and 11:00 and sometimes has running water. They charge four Lempira ($2) for a room with a double bed. We are there with Hollis (how quickly he changed from being Mr. Hayword) and the Lepaterigue team is in the other (slightly nicer). The third team, from Guatemala was supposed to meet us here, but never showed up. Too much rain had left them stranded on the wrong side of a river before they reached the border. We partied and talked together, learning about each others' experiences. The other team has a less ambitious program, concentrating on giving classes and building some desks. Their biggest success stories revolve around literacy students. The discussions turned serious when Hollis explained that the future of the Cornell-in-Central America program is shaky, but all of us have shown such enthusiasm that he now wants to keep it going. We are committed to try together to not let it die (or to at least give a good enough accounting to ensure, as Don Lelo would say, that it gets an honest and decent burial).

Sunday, Aug 8

After the rain last night and our improvised celebration, things are looking normal again this morning. The sun was shining and breakfast was plentiful. We joined our companions at the other hotel (Marina) where we would have been staying if there had not been some mix up in the reservations. (A group of the ever-present *Amigos* were staying there as well.)

The ruins are a couple of miles outside of town. There was a single caretaker occupying a small building at the entrance and collecting a fee. We arrived about the time a chartered DC-3 landed carrying an archeologist from the University of Honduras and a small tour group. We hooked on with them. This was another stroke of luck; we got a far better deal than we could have by wandering around on our own with the little folder we got from the caretaker. The explanations were quite clear and certainly interesting. The professor was able to translate a few of the carvings on the many stone monuments, especially the dates. He also explained the usage of several different (animal and human) sacrificial alters, ball courts, burial grounds, and aqueducts. My personal favorite was a stone stairway where each step was a row of grinning skulls carved in stone. Less than half of the site has been excavated. The tour lasted a good two hours.

Our Milparada team walked back to Hotel Maya for lunch. A doctor from the Amigos was at the next table, iodizing the hotel's boiled water. He got mad when lunch was served at 12:15pm instead of noon. He made his dissatisfaction known by berating a waiter at 12:05pm. The ugly American tourist is not a work of fiction.

After lunch, we roamed through the marketplace. It was very colorful and busy. Scattered among the food vendors, we were accosted by a number of vendors of "ancient sculptures from the ruins" freshly carved from stone or wood. After a couple of rounds of bargaining, I bought a detailed replica of one of the gods carved in a soft wood from a teenager for $1.50.

After short rest and a soda, we climbed into the hotel's *busito* (Jeep station wagon) for our trip home. Doug and Juan started out on top, cooler and less cramped, but a couple of soldiers stopped us and told them to get inside. At one point, we encountered a truck completely turned over, wheels in the air with a clearly drunken driver next to it. We got off at La Entrada, where we once again encountered our vaccinating Amigos at dinner, then caught the late bus to Quimistan. By now our money really was running out. We couldn't talk the driver into taking a detour to Milparada, so we trudged home in the dark.

Don Lelo was exuberant when he greeted us. He had acted as the host of last night's movie from the U.S.I.S. and said everyone enjoyed it. I wish I could have seen the kids react to their first ever movie. Don Lelo and Pedro had been doing more planning for the *comedor* and compiled a census of the children in the village. While we were talking, Doug somehow got Antonio Cruz to take a shower. What a difference it made to see his smiling face shiny and clean.

My cot feels good. We've changed many of our tastes and demands. We actually discussed *Starlac* (powdered milk) as a luxury.

The coming week promises to be a big one with the pressure of trying to finish the *comedor* and have a structure ready for the visitors from San Pedro expected next Sunday. More important to us all is seeing the seventy or so children receiving much needed nutrition on a daily basis.

Mon, Aug 9

Time has become the dominating factor with respect to our work here, and it is obvious that the entire team is aware that efficiency must be maintained at all costs. With this in mind, our labor at the *comedor* today went especially well. We finished the bases (concrete with around the steel pipes) for all four columns. The first one seemed to take forever – our mid-morning progress was discouraging, but somehow we manage to accelerate the work in the afternoon. But we still needed a night shift – with kerosene lantern and flashlights - to finish. Antonio was responsible for part of the delay, as it was necessary to convince him that Doug's method was more practical than his ideas in this case. The girls have taken over the majority of the cooking and dishwashing duties so the boys can spend more time working on the *comedor*. For some inexplicable reason, everyone seems confident that together we can finish the *comedor*, even though that appears to be an impossible amount of work for eight people in eight days.

We are all tired and ready for a quick shower and sleep.

Tues, Aug 10

Rejoice and raise a column – and that's just what we did today (the boys and helpers from the town). It certainly was a real work day.

We were able to borrow wooden forms for the columns from Quimistan. We positioned them carefully and used scrap wood to brace them securely. Pouring them went slowly. We had to lean two ladders against opposite sides of the forms and hand the cement up in varnish cans, one gallon at a time. One of the workers on the ladders poured the cement, the other pushed/stirred it with a pole to try to prevent any air pockets from forming. We completed all four columns by dusk.

At the same time, we began work on the kitchen, which is a very substantial lean-to extending off the back side of the *comedor*. This work entailed cutting large timber for supports and roof poles. Also, our helpers brought an oxcart full of pine needles to make adobe blocks for the ovens. The roof of the kitchen was made from the red tiles which are used on most of the local buildings.

As the columns went up, the girls were debarking the logs for the kitchen's roof with machetes. This scandalous behavior made them the primary subject for gossip in town. The girls quickly became proficient in handling the long knives, and have blisters on their hands that attest to their labors.

Don Lelo left today. He certainly looked tired. This project has been hard on him – trying to get everything managed and coordinated. He left with the promise that he would return on Friday and bring us more bread and Starlac.

Our food situation is rather poor – we are mostly down to rice and beans, along with oatmeal for breakfast. Dona Candida made us some bread today – yum, yum, so good.

Mary and Melissa met a drunk in Quimistan when they went to get our mail – and were, of course, deeply scandalized. The sounded like they had never seen a drunk before; I wonder what college campuses they have been on. Only half of the team members got mail this week. Those who didn't are jealous. Maybe our families have stopped writing because they think we will be on our way home before the next round of letters would reach us.

Wed, Aug 11

Yesterday was exhausting. We got moving in "record time" today – finishing breakfast at 8:15, which gave our helpers an hour's head start. No matter, they started working on the kitchen without us. We started making measurements and calculations for the A-frame trusses. We had to do this carefully -- we have no allowance for wastage once we start sawing.

We were just starting to put the first one together when the Quimistan school arrived in force to visit the gringos and the school. Their company included seven teachers, one hundred ten kids and the area supervisor. There was a short ceremony at the school, for which my guitar and I were pressed into service. It featured the Milparada students singing "Esta Tierra" and the Spanish translation of the "Star Spangled Banner" by a chorus of Quimistecos. Afterwards, the visiting girls played volleyball while the Milparada boys won a soccer game. My students came through again!

Meanwhile, the boys kept discovering things we had overlooked in our truss plans – so after a picnic lunch with all the school children, we returned to the drawing boards. After laying everything out, we did completely assemble one of the trusses. That leaves three for tomorrow. The girls also spent most of the afternoon in physical labor, helping with the kitchen construction.

We have set a deadline of Saturday for getting the entire roof up. It is obvious that everything won't be finished on our scheduled date for leaving. We still have more than half of the floor to pour and haven't started on the tables. I don't want to leave without finishing what we started. The other team members agree that it would be good for a couple of us stay an extra week, but they all have reservations and commitments they can't change. My plan to sightsee on my own can be adjusted; I'd rather be here. I could stay by myself. Marcos was hanging around and immediately invited me to stay at his house. I thanked him but said I didn't want to cause anyone trouble so he should ask his parents first. "My father is away for two weeks, so I am the man of the house. You can sleep on my brother's hammock in the kitchen." We have a deal, though I'll try to check with his mother tomorrow.

To bed early, hoping we can get more done tomorrow.

Friday the 13ᵗʰ

Yesterday was just another full, tiring day of labor. We didn't finish until after dark. We assembled the other three trusses. Today, we put up the beams in anticipation of raising the trusses tomorrow. They are firmly anchored to the pipes that run through the center of the columns,

Lunch was an event that will long stick in our minds. We were all able to be present for the first day of operation of the *comedor*. The event drew a large crowd of beaming parents to the school. It was a very satisfying and emotional sight to see the whole school eating full plates of wholesome food (tortillas, beans, bulgar wheat meal, and powdered milk). Soon they will be adding fresh vegetables from the school garden. I helped out by pouring milk.

I overheard Antonio saying, "Milk is for babies."

"Do I look like a baby to you? And Douglas, is he a baby?"

"No."

"We drink milk every day. You know that; you've watched our dinners. Milk makes the bones grow big and strong."

There were no more comments about milk. Many of the kids were skeptical and cautious in tasting the wheat. It looked like a blob of thick oatmeal. They were poking at it with their spoons and looking around for someone else who was eating theirs. Our girls did some prodding/encouraging and once they tasted it they smiled and ate it all. No admonitions about the "clean plate club" needed here.

Irma has demonstrated that she is an excellent choice for permanent head cook. She is a responsible and organized person – the food was ready right on time and she had her helpers organized to serve efficiently. The only logistical problem came at the end when the line of children were all trying to wash their plates, cups and silverware at the single water tap – washing with soap and rinsing over mud.

We were all very encouraged and charged up to complete all the preliminaries so we can raise the roof tomorrow. I don't feel so tired tonight.

Saturday, August 14

Today was our biggest single construction feat. Each truss weighs at least six hundred pounds, so in lifting them up ten feet and securing them to the brackets mounted on the beams, any slip up could cause a major injury. We had a crew of ten men eagerly helping us today.

All of my work shirts are dirty, damp with old sweat and stink. So today, I worked shirtless like Ed and Doug. Two of the younger men also took off their shirts. I was conspicuously white. The remaining men sensibly stayed with the sun protection of shirts and hats. I think I got by without a significant sunburn.

We spent most of the first hour discussing how to manage the task. We ended up with Ed and Doug on top of the beam on one side and me on the other. The men would push from below using boards to help. We temporarily nailed a couple of "handle" boards to the truss to provide a steady grip. The helpers first lifted one end up to Doug and Ed who pulled it over far enough so that the other side could be raised inside the far beam for me to grab. One of the men came up the ladder on my side with the end. Then we could inch it into its centered position. Then one man on each side could nail the truss to a bracket while the other kept the truss from wobbling over. Then we'd switch roles, while a second bracket secured the other side of the truss to each beam. We got all four trusses in place by 1:00pm. They still looked precariously balanced, so we helped Doug get them secured with a ridgepole before taking a late lunch.

During the afternoon we got the crossbeams in place and put on the first couple of roofing sheets. The girls did our laundry – bless their souls.

Word is out that I am staying longer. The reaction has been flattering.

I had a long talk with Antonio Machado. He expects the *comedor* to fail when we leave. "There is no community spirit here. Everyone will fight for any materials we leave behind." He is still mad at us for starting the floor before the roof was completed to protect it from rain, even though the completed portion of the floor hardened smoothly. Yet he continues to work harder than anyone else and was beaming ear-to-ear watching the kids eat their first meal. He offered me food and lodging for the rest of my stay. He has had a good year and has more than enough corn set aside to last until after the harvest. Last year he had to sell some of his corn in advance at eight *Lempira* per *quintal* ($4.00 per 100 pounds) and then buy some back at twelve *Lempira*. He said that he got off easy compared to those who sold right after the harvest. I would also have my own bed. (It would be better than what Marcos' family could offer.) He was surprised, but understanding when I said I had already accepted Marco's offer and didn't want to offend his family by choosing somewhere else.

This afternoon, I wrote a last letter home:

Sat. Aug 14

Dear family,

We finally got most of the material we need for the comedor and added a night shift by Coleman lantern to make up for lost time. This week, we've put up 4 cement columns and made 4 large A frame trusses and various cross-beams - all of which we got set up today. Also, we got the CARE food Thurs. afternoon, so the comedor started service yesterday. The committee (which we set up) cooked in our kitchen and served in the school until the permanent structure is finished. To add to the confusion, Wed. the entire Quimistan school (115 strong) came to visit us.

Also, there's been a slight change in my plans. I'm going to stay over an extra week, living with the family of some very good friends, to tie up a few loose ends and to pave the way for next year's team to work in another town. This means I'll lose all my tourist time in Guatemala and Mexico, but the itinerary from El Paso on is still correct/

I'm still having the time of my life and am none the worse for wear (except I've lost a little weight, but your home cooking will take care of that when I return).

I almost forgot, we went to Copan last week and really enjoyed it, although the trip was something else (up to 16 people in and on a Jeep panel truck).

Love to all, Dick

P.S. Got the grades, what a lovely surprise.

Tonight, the team celebrated by going into Quimistan and partying with soda or beer.

Sunday, August 15

We got a late start this morning. The asbestos roofing sheets are brittle and have to be handled delicately to keep from crumbling the edges or cracking them while fastening them to the crossbeams with special screws and rubber washers. Doug is doing all of the skilled work on top. Ed and I fed him the sheets from below. We got the roof half finished and ran out of the screws.

Meanwhile the locals finished the shelters for the three latrines. They are now complete with hinged doors.

Tomorrow will be our last full day together. Our mood tonight is a strange mixture of happiness and melancholy. We are proud of how much we have accomplished. We can honestly assert that the construction program in Milparada was successful and that the original intentions were more than fulfilled. The comedor is our greatest pride, but we also had successes with the desk building and literacy programs. At times the work was slow and frustrating due to inexperience, delays, etc. As a team, we have worked through many problems and supported each other. We have had our share of good luck, plus a tremendous amount of help from our good friends Nelly, Rafael and Don Lelo. Our major work is complete, and the *comedor* is operating. We know new problems will arise. There is no guarantee that they will all be solved, or even that the "*Comite Milparada Hacia el Progreso*" won't collapse. However, the outlook is hopeful. Don Lelo will carry the torch for the project after we are gone.

The melancholy mainly comes from thinking about the conditions that the villages continue to endure. The nurses provided the people with the best medical care they have ever had, and our involvement almost undoubtedly saved at least two lives. But that help was only temporary. We haven't succeeded in making their future health prospects any better. The health classes were a disappointing failure. Looking back, we can only question ourselves as to whether it would have been better to a plan to visit every home to issue personal invitations, or more importantly, to be sure we knew all the people and that they knew us well enough to come to our classes. The nurses' limited command of Spanish made them hesitant in such approaches at times. We probably left them too much on their own. Maybe having Juan or Ed, with their complete language fluency, would have helped. Certainly, we realize how foreign health classes are to the women of Milparada.

We were saddened by many things: When women wipe their children's nose on the shawls used to wrap the children; when babies urinate on their mother's lap; when barefoot children and adults romp through the human and animal waste plentiful in the soil; when women fear a boy as good as dead when he has obtained a gash near a male gland which might impair his masculinity; when houses are dark and close inside from lack of windows and keeping the doors closed. Yet, surely these very sad living conditions are the norm in much of rural Honduras. Children grow up in an uncomfortable world, as will their children in turn. To ask these people to change is asking much. We must realize that if the women of the village had, for instance, been able to "modernize" to the extent that daily chores took less of their time, they would likely be dismayed at what to do with extra time required to take sanitary precautions.

The needs of the area are so great. The government has limited financial resources, and is putting a strong emphasis on education to reduce illiteracy. But to significantly improve life in the countryside, they also will need many more doctors, better roads, electricity and higher-yield agriculture. All phases of life are inter-related. Our feeding center, latrines and other efforts are just a tiny drop in the bucket. Still our efforts have been greatly appreciated.

We have made many good friends and great memories that will last a lifetime. This summer has given each of us more than we would have ever dreamed.

Monday, August 16

There is no water running in Milparada this morning, as the team prepares to leave. Ed made a final early trip to San Pedro to procure enough cushioned screws to finish the roof and bolts that will be needed for the tables.

Packing of cooking utensils will have to be postponed because we have to use them – but suitcases could be packed right away. It seemed strange to see the bookshelf emptied and cots strewn with our worldly belongings. Mary and Melissa repeated a performance from the first week – going to the river to wash clothes.

Many people came for medicine today, maybe wanting to stock up for a long hard year ahead. At any rate, we've run out of aspirins, cough medicine and medicine for grippe. On the positive side, our team was able to leave the schoolteacher a first aid kit consisting basically of gauze, cotton, tape, mercurochrome, Phisohex and a thermometer. This is very basic, but it may be the start for the village. Melissa selected *Profesora* Maria Luisa as the custodian of the kit because she is a central figure in town, well-known and respected; she is in contact with all the families through their kids, and she is educated enough to use the first aid kit wisely.

Irma and Dona Laura prepared the second *comedor* meal. Today was a special meal including tomatoes and our leftover brown bread along with beans, tortillas, our sardines and milk. During the meal, Rafael drove up in a Jeep with Ed, the screws and soap for CARE for *comedor* dishwashing. It is always good to see Rafael, though today his visit was brief. The sky looked like rain and a rumor was going around that we would dance in the evening.

After lunch, we went back to working on the roof of the *comedor*. The rain held off, so work continued until almost dark. We still haven't got it finished. I hope I don't have to climb around on the roof to complete the job after Doug leaves.

Mary had brought a bag of plastic trinkets for the children. This afternoon's recess resembled a mob-scene as Trinchi, Sue and Mary passed out the goodies.

The water returned through the pipes in time to fix a late dinner. The rain came while we were eating. By the time we were finished, the dance was ready to begin. As Pedro said, "one more memory for us of Milparada." The Milparada gents kept the four Cornell girls whirling. The fellows danced with all the local women of all sizes. Pedro supplied soda and beer. Don Lelo was there with a sad and tired face, but wouldn't dance. After the dance broke up, we took our long awaited showers and went to bed. The alarm is set for 5:00am – hoping to finish the roof in the morning, along with packing and farewells.

Tues. August 17

We got up at 5:00am and ate a breakfast of left-over everything. Melissa gave me the bottle of vitamin pills for me to take every day. She is concerned about my health if I "go native" for the coming week.

By 6:15am the boys were working on the roof and five townsmen were working on the clay oven for the kitchen. Meanwhile, the girls packed the team's cookware, etc. amid a swarm of people. Nelly arrived in her pickup with Chito at 10:00am. Chito helped the girls load it with our cots and gear.

We finished the roof at 10:30am, shortly before the VW bus arrived. I carried my suitcase and guitar to Marcos' house while the rest of the luggage is stuffed in the VW. By the time we finished preparing for the departure, the grouchy owner of the boys' house had inspected it and scavenged loose ends.

We were surrounded by people with sad eyes as the team members said their good-byes. At least a dozen men took the morning off to see the team off. The school children were given an extra recess during the departure. Pedro's catch phrase is no longer "*mucho trabajo*" (much work), but "*Nos faltan mucho cuando ustedes se van.*" (We are missing a lot when you all go away.) One former patient came by with all of her children to say good-bye and brought a gift of eggs. The question they all asked is "When will you return?"

I said my own farewells. It was hard to express my personal appreciation and admiration for my teammates. Each has contributed to the fabric of this summer, and we have added our own pattern to the weave. We believe our patterns have strengthened Milparada's fabric. They know they have a committee, some desks, and the *comedor*. Antonio has learned how to give his wife her daily insulin injection, so she no longer has to walk to Pinalejo for it. They have learned some English words, which serve as a source of pride.

By 11:30am, everyone else had left. Tonight, the rest of the team will be entertained at the Swansons'. Tomorrow they will scatter on their way home. I am left alone and in charge of finishing our work. The school children were served their lunch in the school and I joined Marcos at his house for a saucer of black beans in their own soup (in a brown cup) and two tortillas with salt, followed by a drink of water.

I spent the afternoon re-working all the table legs. They were supposed to arrive cut to the correct dimensions, but no two were the same length. Jacobo Hernandez helped with the sawing when he came in from the fields. It was slow going with our dull saws. At 4:40pm I left for Quimistan to borrow a whetstone to sharpen the two saws. Charlie gave me a ride back. Antonio and four helpers laid the final third of the floor. Antonio was still smoothing the cement with his wooden trowel when I left for supper.

I discovered that Lelo had locked the team's latrine and didn't give me a key. It didn't cause any real problem. I just used the teachers'. I wonder why in the world any one would lock a latrine, especially one sitting in the backyard of an empty house.

Dinner was served at 6:30pm. The food was the same as lunch but with a cup of coffee with a heaping teaspoon of sugar. Senora de Hernandez offered to fix me extra food, since the gringos ate more. I declined, "Thank you, no. I want you to treat me the same as though I was one of your family."

Marcos' mother, Senora Margareta de Hernandez, is one of the women who has volunteered to help cook in the *comedor*. She is forty-five, and shows signs of having lived a hard life. As we visited during and after dinner, she straightened me out on who's who in the family.

Her husband, Julian Hernandez is forty. They moved here from Santa Rosa de Copan shortly after they got married. Julian is away in the mountains for two weeks. He took Lena, their mule, with him to earn money cutting wood with his son.

Her oldest daughter is twenty-eight and lives near the river with her husband and their four children. She gave birth to Bartito when she was sixteen. Margareta made it clear where he belongs. "I raised him, so he's mine."

Her second daughter is married. She doesn't live near here.

Tina is Julian's oldest daughter. She is twenty. Tina does most of the cooking and housekeeping.

Carlos is Marcos' eighteen year old brother. He spends most of his time living in the lumber camp in Cordaderos. He earns one Lempira ($0.50) per day; he also gets fed his meals – so it is a good job. He brings the family some money or gifts whenever he comes home.

Marcos is fourteen.

Bartito Nineco is twelve. He spent three years in school, passing the first two grades. Now he is a helper in the fields, but he doesn't have shoes yet. He definitely looks and acts as though he is Marcos' little brother. Bartito has eagerly helped the team in digging the latrine hole and debarking logs for the *comedor* kitchen. Marcos confided to me that "Bartito has worms."

Delia Hernandez is twelve and in third grade. She is a good student. At least when I'm around, she is very quiet and demure.

Jorge Nineco is Bartito's six year old cousin. I presume that means the second daughter gave birth to him before she got married. He is very quiet for a little guy.

Claudio is their three year old toddler. He is pant less. He bulging belly shows that he already has worms.

The baby, Jesus is eighteen months old.

The household also includes a number of animals: a cat, six dogs (four are recent puppies), two pigs, five hens and a rooster. The animals eat kitchen waste and whatever they grub for themselves. The hens lay only one or two eggs a week. Delia sells them to the store for five centavos a piece.

By 9:00pm the rest of the family had retired to the bedroom and Marcos had shown me how to hang the hammock. It is time to go to sleep.

Wed. August 18

The hammock was comfortable, but it'll take some getting used to sleeping with both my head and feet a good eighteen inches higher than my butt. The noises were different too. The hens had come in through holes in the kitchen wall and settled under the table for the night. I could hear occasional clucking as I drifted off to sleep.

Morning came too soon. I woke at 4:00 am. Tina was in the kitchen making a fire in the stove. By 4:15 was been joined by Senora de Hernandez and Bartito. Bartito was grinding corn. The two women started making tortillas and coffee. Everybody is up by 4:30, so that's when I got up and put away the hammock. Marcos and I walked to the nearest water tap, with Jorge trailing along. I shaved and we all rinsed off our hands and faces.

We ate breakfast at 5:15. Breakfast consisted of two tortillas for the workers – the small fry got one apiece. Today they were fried in some lard thrown on the stove top. That was a special treat in my honor. Everyone except the baby had a cup of strong coffee with a heaping spoonful of sugar.

At 5:45, the mother, and Bartito left for the *Tobacalero* in Quimistan (taking a bundle of tortillas for lunch). Delia was cleaning up the kitchen before school. Both the floor and yard are swept daily to clean up after animals. Marcos wrapped his lunch tortillas in a cloth and headed off to the corn field with a gourd of water and his machete. I went to work on the *comedor*. Tina stayed to take care of the little ones. She would have lunch ready for me and the kids at noon.

I started work by tediously sharpening the saw. We did have a little turpentine to clean off the sticky sap. I was soon joined by Jacobo Hernandez. He is twenty-four and is just starting his term as the *Alcalde Auxiliar*. He is a good soccer player and puts on an air of arrogance. Prior to today, most of our conversations have consisted of him teasing me about women. With the one saw, one hand augur and two wrenches, the two of us spent most of the day assembling the frames for the tables. The final product will be three fourteen-foot picnic tables with benches attached. We are making them from eight-inch wide planks of two-inch thick rough pine stock. The wood is green and heavy. Each table needs three frames consisting of legs and supports for the top planks and benches. The parts are bolted together. They will be excessively substantial.

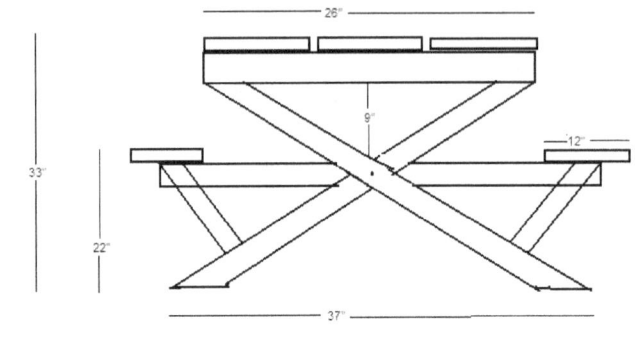

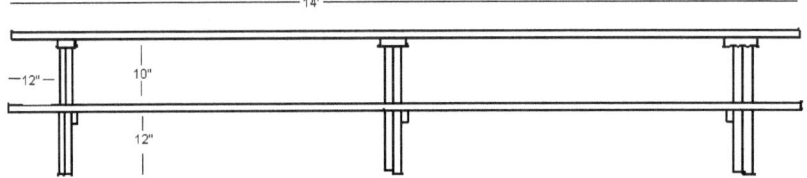

Figure 7. Plans for tables

As we worked together, Jacobo switched to address me with the familiar *"tu,"* instead to the formal *"usted"* that he had always used when the full team was present. I took that as a signal that I am being accepted as a friend and no longer an outsider.

We got all nine frames finished by mid-afternoon. I'm afraid that two of them look a little crooked, so the bench on one side will be a little higher than the other. I hope nobody minds. Tomorrow we'll nail on the tops and benches.

Meanwhile, Antonio and a helper laid the rest of the cement floor and other townsmen finished an enlarged version of the standard adobe stove. It has two oil-drum lids for the cooking surface and a wider than normal platform. Antonio worked until dusk finishing the floor.

Our work was interrupted at 10:30 am by a visitor in a pickup truck. He got out and looked around for a few minutes before approaching me and asking for the address of Cornell. He had heard about us while he was in San Pedro and wanted to ask for a team to come to his home town of Aldeas. It turns out that Aldeas is not far from Lepaterigue and Tegucigalpa. Driving over to Milparada was quite a bit out of his way, so I felt quite flattered by the visit. I thanked him for his interest, but told him that only a few students could come each summer and the planning for next year had already started, so that it would probably be at least two years before we could get a team assigned to his town, but we would appreciate his letter and see what we could do. I dug out the official address for the project and he drove off.

I also noticed that the owner of the boys' house was hard at work attacking our cement floor with a pickaxe. Jacobo explained most of the people think that a dirt floor is best because it absorbs the rain that drips through the roof along with spit and spills. The cement floor would leave puddles and be too hard to clean. Our presence hasn't changed their understanding of sanitation and health. Tradition continues to exert a more powerful force.

Lunch was the same small meal as yesterday.

Marcos had killed an iguana, about three feet long, on his way back from the fields. He was proud of providing a special treat for dinner. I had to admit that I had never tasted iguana meat. He let me know that that the tail is the best part; it is dropped directly on the stove top to be grilled. Dinner was a slightly larger meal: two tamales (just balls of cornmeal wrapped in a husk and boiled), four bites of iguana meat (it tasted like very greasy dark chicken meat), one tortilla with salt, and a cup of sugared coffee. There is no chance for any privacy in the house, so I've decided to leave the vitamins in my suitcase. It is only for a week.

While the women clean up the kitchen, Marcos and I took a stroll around the village. We started with some more of my questions, this time about personal hygiene. People take a bath once or twice a week, and wash their hands and face every morning. Soap is a luxury, it is used only when bathing for a special occasion and for washing clothes (not dishes). Most villagers generally use store bought soap, but a few people (like Sebastiano) make their own. Making soap takes a long time and not everybody has the raw ingredients. The soap is made by boiling tallow from a cow with lye and a few other things for three days. It is always made on a fire outside because it smells so much. Men get a hair cut every six to eight weeks. His father goes to Quimistan and pays fifty centavos ($0.25) for hair cut and shave. Marcos uses the local barber, Senor Cruz, because he only charges 20 centavos. Women comb and brush their hair daily, but never get it cut.

Marcos perked up when we saw twelve year old Julia across the way, and asked if I liked her. I figured that he is more than a little smitten with her, so I give him a polite answer.

"She is a nice girl and yes she is beautiful."

"Would you like her to be your girlfriend?"

"She is too little for me." I quickly realized that I had used the wrong word. I should have said "too young."

Marcos was laughing at me. "She's little and you are big so you won't fit. Huh?"

I tried to explain about wanting my girlfriend to be an equal partner, someone with common experiences to talk about. It was too late. His teenage mind was stuck on body parts.

We returned to his house before it got dark. Senora de Hernadez had set their kerosene "candle" on the table but not lit it. They only bring it out when they have guests. Usually they just move a little kindling to the front of the stove to provide a little evening light. I said the fire was sufficient. If I needed more light for anything I could use my flashlight.

There are no cabinets or dressers. The family's property is arrayed on a few shelves. The inventory consists of three spoons, a teapot, a coffee pot with strainer, two cooking pots (one of them has a lid), one small frying pan, two glasses, two dinner plates and five saucers, a salt dish, five cups, three tin cans (used for storage), six bottles (with corn cob corks), six paper bags, some gourds for dipping water, a grindstone for corn, a woven basket eighteen inches in diameter, four gourd canteens (to take water to drink in the fields), three machetes, the net hammock, one homemade broom, two burlap bags, the kerosene "candle", an iron (heated by putting embers inside), one kitchen knife and one old almanac. They share a metal pail with their next-door neighbor for hauling water.

Marcos told me he has two sets of clothes. They keep the clothes they aren't wearing under mattresses on their beds.

Bed at 8:30pm.

Thurs. August 19

Today started the same as yesterday

There were no helpers around when I started work at the *comedor*. I took off the forms from the columns. I had some anxiety when I started. If there were any flaws in our poured concrete they would be obvious and have to be repaired. The columns came out fine, smooth and hard with no obvious air holes. I had them down and stacked by 10:00am. About then, some helpers arrived and we put the tables together. I am moving slower today. The local diet is leaving me constantly hungry and low on energy. I remember the comments we had made about how much time our helpers spent just standing around. I wish I could take those comments back, now that I've walked in their shoes for a couple of days. The *comedor* was now complete and ready for business!

Unfortunately Irma was gone for the day, so there was no school lunch. I'm afraid that meant that half the kids had no lunch at all today. It also shows how fragile the Committee is. There was no plan is place for a back-up cook when Irma is not available.

My own lunch was a toasted ear of sweet corn on the cob (roasted in its husk) and a saucer of rice and beans. It tasted good; I just wish there was more.

I spent the next few hours working on a map of the village. I used marching band paces six-steps-to-five yards so the scale would be reasonably accurate. I must have looked strange to the locals, marching around by myself. The map turned out looking pretty good, if I do say so myself

Around 3:00pm, I walked to the post office in Quimistan. The only thing waiting for our team was two copies of a letter from Don Lelo that didn't contain any news

I swung by the Tobacalero. It is just a large covered cement slab where about fifty people, mostly women and children, were sorting and bundling tobacco leaves for shipment to the factory in San Pedro Sula. They are paid fifty centavos at the end of the day. I walked back with Senora de Hernandez and Bartito.

Tonight's dinner was a saucer of beans, one tortilla and coffee. Bed 8:15.

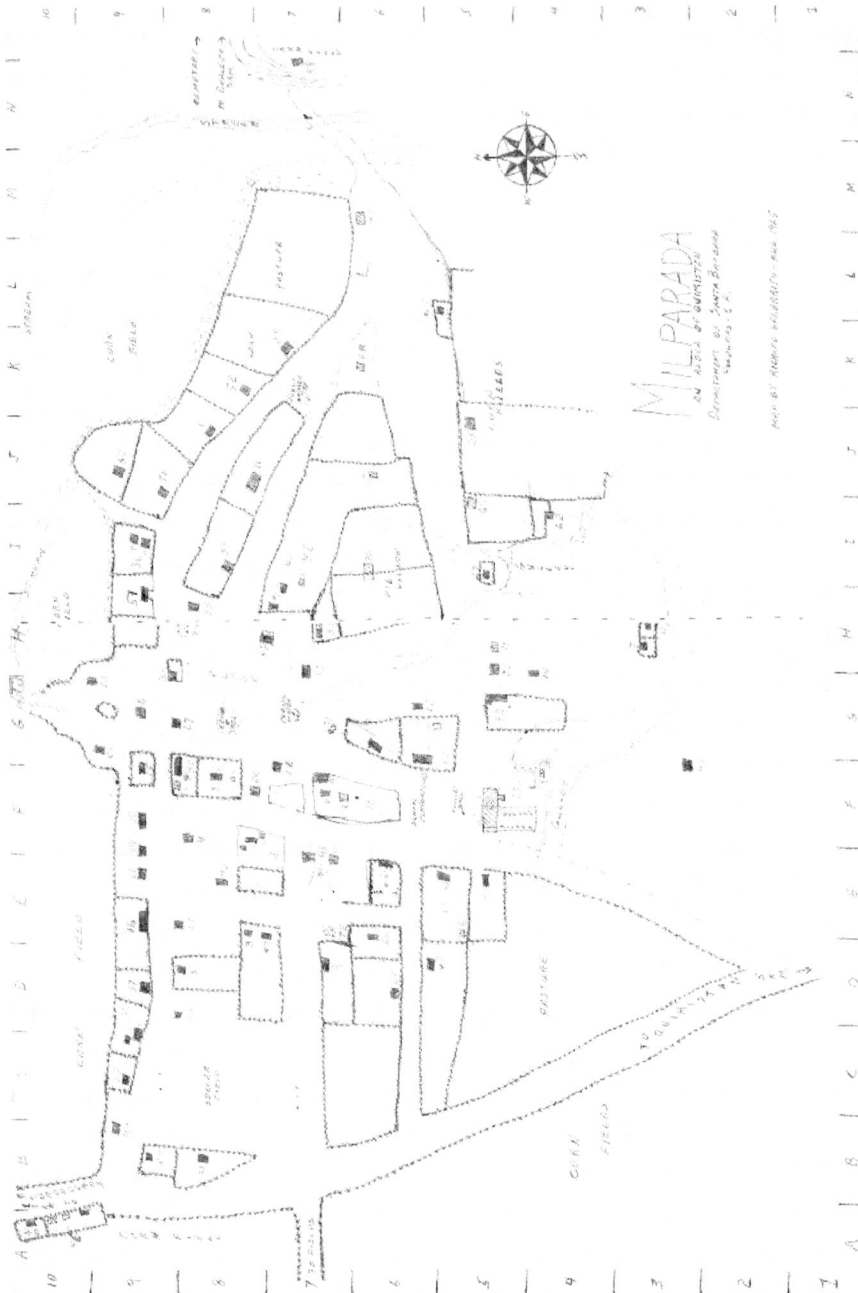

Figure 8. Map of Milparada

Fri. August 20

Senora de Hernandez and Delia were up at 3:40am. They tried not to disturb me, but the location of the hammock made that a hopeless cause. Delia is walking to Cordaderos to sell *"chica"* (chewing gum) on their market day. She buys the *chica* in Quimistan with the money she gets for the eggs, then the young men who work for the lumber company will buy it from a pretty young girl for a nice markup.

Our breakfast was refried beans with rice and coffee.

The impact of the team leaving really hit me today. Everyone I encountered talked about wanting the same group back, how much they would miss us, and couldn't I stay longer. Eduardo DuBon has just gotten back from a week of work on a coffee farm. He was almost crying as he apologized for not making it back to see the team off and for missing a week of literacy classes. He was eager to get to work – volunteering to finish whatever needed to be done. We devoted the morning to gathering firewood for the *comedor* kitchen with four other townsmen. We gathered enough to last for more than a month.

School lunch was served in the completed *comedor*. We had forty-five students on the three long tables, legs dangling while they enjoyed a balanced meal. Watching them sent chills up my spine. They looked so happy and full of promise. My lunch with Tina was cold rice and beans.

This afternoon, I supplemented the map with a census. Armando DuBon helped me by supplying the names and number of people living in most of the houses. After school let out, Juancito Hernandez walked with me and filled in the remaining gaps. They each volunteered negative opinions and stories about a number of their neighbors. Based on our count, Milparada has a total population of three hundred ninety five people living in sixty-five households. All but five of the houses are *"bararequé"*, local adobe plastered against a wood frame, with tile or thatched straw roofs. One of the others is Manuel DuBon's frame house-store, and the rest are *"jacales"*, made of upright poles lashed together.

When Marcos came back from the field I showed him the map. He quickly figured out how to read it, then wanted to know how I made it. I showed him by making a map of their house and furniture. (He insisted that I draw in the *gato* (cat) and *perros* (dogs).

Dinner tonight was beans, flour tortillas (we had run out of corn from the last harvest and flour is cheaper at this time of year). I got one bite of lamb meat in my saucer of beans. We finished off the meal with the usual strong, sugared coffee.

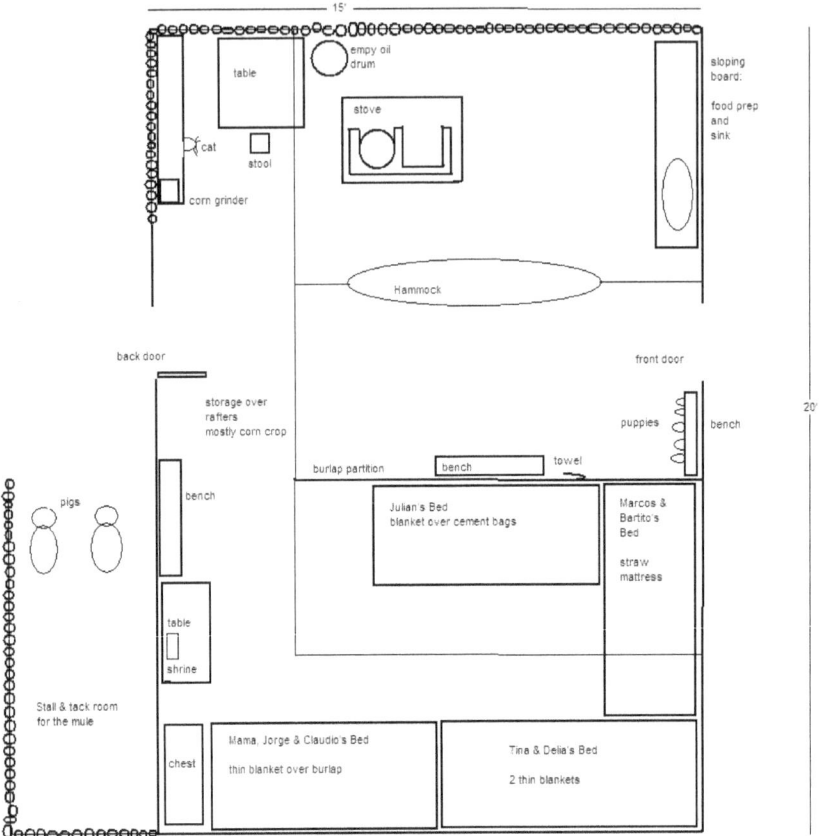

Figure 9. Marco's house

     Since the construction work is finished, the evening talk focused on my leaving. I have to go to Chiquila tomorrow to do some ground work for next year's possible project. I invited Marcos to come with me. I'll be able to spend all day Sunday with the family before leaving on Monday. Marcos and Bartito said they don't want me to leave unless I take them with me. I wish I could, but it is impossible. (I have three more years of living in a dorm room and can barely support myself. There is no way I could take care of them in the United States. There is also no way that I would qualify as a sponsor to get either of them a visa.) I can't even tell them if I will ever be able to come back to Honduras. Both boys were crying when they went to bed. There are tears in my eyes as I write this. They are such good kids. They deserve more than I can give them.

Sat. August 21

     We were up at 4:30am. Breakfast was a saucer of beans, a tortilla and coffee.

     Marcos and I walked to Quimistan and caught a bus to Chiquila. We arrived there at 9:15am. The male school teacher wasn't there. The woman teacher took a recess break to walk me around the site for the new school. She and the Auxilary Mayor had a clear idea of what space they wanted. They were looking ahead to a future when the school could handle grades one through six.   It didn't take long to draw up a floor plan.

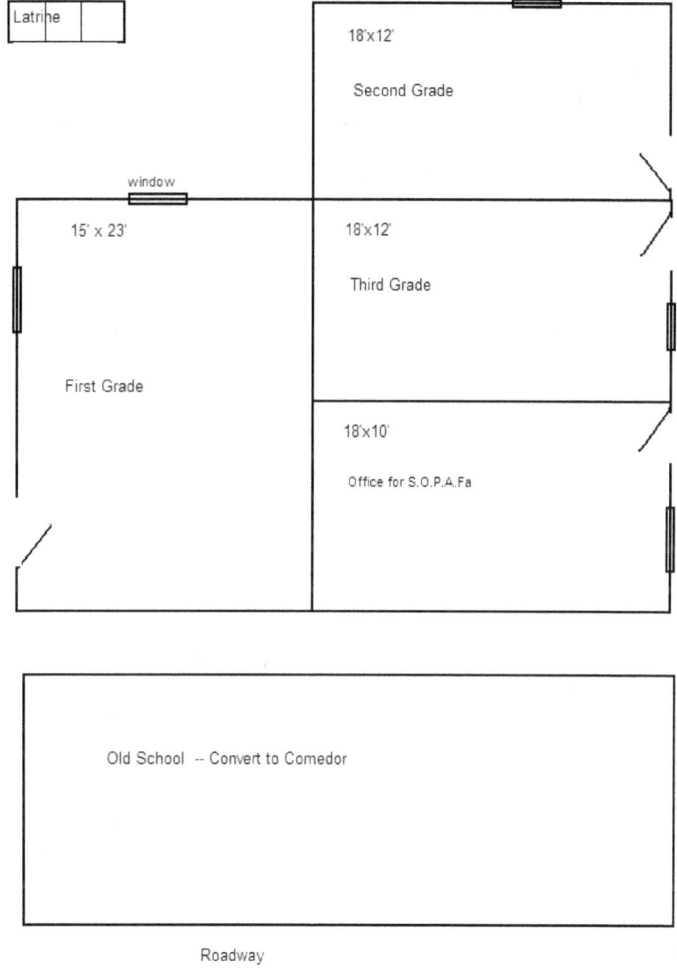

Figure 10. Plan for Chiquila school

The teacher asked one of her older students, Diego, to show us around the village. Marcos beamed when I introduced him as my little brother. There wasn't much to see, so he took us to the bathing spot for males. He said the girls' bathing spot is upstream on the other end of the village and the men are not allowed to go near there. The bathing spot was a short stretch where the river narrowed with the road forming a high bank on one side. The water was murky enough that I could see the bottom. Diego slipped off his shirt and pants and dove in. I had a quick image of myself diving in and hitting my head on a rock, so I cautiously walked down to a large rock, stripped to my underpants and slipped into the water. It was marvelously cool and refreshing; especially since it had been four days since my last bath. Marcos was still standing on the bank.

"Come in, the water is cool," I called out to him.

He shook his head and said "No."

I was surprised by his shyness. "Why not? It will feel good."

"I can't swim." Of course not, there is no place near Milparada where the water is more than a few inches deep.

I stood up. The water only came to my belly button. "Look it is fine."

Marcos came down and joined us. We enjoyed almost a half-hour of splashing around and relaxing. (Diego knew exactly where the only hole was that was deep enough for diving.)

Our bus ride back was unusually crowded - thirty-nine passengers inside a school bus built for twenty with two more men on top. In Quimistan, we had a big lunch at La Flecha then stopped by the store. It had no postage stamps and no corn available for purchase, so I settled on a can of sardines that Marcos said his family would like.

In the afternoon, we took our machetes and gathered firewood for their house. A little later Marcos' father, Julian, came home. He looks just like "Juan Valdez" of the coffee ads, especially since he was leading his mule Lena. He had done his day of assigned helping early on, but nothing more with the team, even though he has three children who will use it. He was very concerned that we would not stay long enough and asked, "When are you going to finish the *comedor*?" He has a fatalistic attitude about life in general. He doesn't think he can do anything to improve his lot, and expects nothing to change for his children." I asked him why he thought the team came here. "To do and to know us." He has had a successful trip and came home with enough money to buy his wife a new dress.

Dinner tonight was boiled plantains, beans and coffee. It is my last night in Milparada. It is going to be hard to say good-bye. We talked longer tonight and didn't go to bed until 9:00pm.

Sunday, August 22

The parents were up at 5:00am, the rest of us got up at 5:30am. Our breakfast was a roasted plantain and coffee.

At 6:30am, Julian, Marcos, Bartito and I walked to the *milpa* for the first harvest of corn. We carefully selected the largest, ripest ears. We returned at 8:30am with both burlap bags full of corn, plus one ripe squash. Then the whole family sat around the main room husking the corn. The mood was marvelously warm and cheerful. Julian declared a few ears to be too green for storage. Those ears were thrown on the stove and roasted. Each of the "workers" got one. Mine was sweet and absolutely delicious – the best-tasting corn I have ever had. We piled the husks and silk out back for the pigs to eat.

At 10:30am we had celebratory lunch: a saucer of soup with a small piece of meat plus rice dumped into the broth, the squash, a plantain, a fresh corn tortilla, the can of sardines and coffee. I left my better pair of Levis as a parting gift. The legs are too long for Julian, but he said that Carlos will prize them.

After lunch I headed off toward the plaza. It was a slow trip, saying good-bye to everyone on the way. Marian (Juancito's mother) stopped me on the way and insisted I join them for lunch. We had some beans wrapped in a tortilla and a cup of coffee). One of the neighbors gave me a cake of homemade soap wrapped in a corn husk. The Machados' insisted that I join them for lunch; this one was pineapple, a tortilla and coffee. When I got to the school, *Profesor* Jacobo gave me one of the baskets he had woven.

Marcos, Bartito, and all of the third grade boys escorted me to Quimistan. They argued over the "privilege" of carrying my bag and guitar. It was an emotional hard walk. On one hand, the love and appreciation the people showered on me felt great. On the other hand the boys kept asking when would I be back and couldn't I stay longer. A big part of me wanted to turn around and stay here. I know I would be welcomed with open arms. I thought about what it would be like, and know that it would get boring for me and turn into a disappointment for them. Their biggest need is for better medical care. I don't have those skills. I thought about becoming a doctor, but I don't have the stomach for it. I would be a lousy farmer. I don't have the capital to set up a business. I couldn't think of anything more that I could do to help the villagers. My future depends on returning to Cornell and completing my degree.

I caught a ride to Cofradia and spent the night with Nelly. We had a big dinner and warm conversation.

Monday, August 23

We got up at 5:00am and enjoyed a big breakfast with Nelly. She dropped me off at Swansons' in San Pedro. That let me get a real, hot shower bath and change to my city clothes before the stores opened for business.

At the SASHA (Honduras's national airline) office in the Hotel Columbia, I got my airplane ticket to Guatemala City and my exit visa. It is a short flight over the mountains on a DC-3. Today's flight was full, so I'll have to wait until Wednesday. That is still quicker than taking buses through Tegucigalpa and San Salvador. And since I have free housing here, I'll save money by flying.

I have a couple of days to kill. I started with an overdue haircut; a hot lathered shave was included in the basic charge. Next I looked up Don Lelo and had a long lunch with him at Vicente's. Lunch included three cold *Tecate* beers. This afternoon I paid a visit on John Moran at the CARE office to report on our successes and thank him for all his help.

When I returned to Swansons' for dinner, Doug and Jim (a member of the Lepaterigue team) were there. They had spent the week snorkeling at some islands off the coast. They had stayed in a resort and enjoyed the life of rich American tourists. It sounded like a great time.

Tuesday, August 24

Swanson gave me a tour of his cigarette factory. The main section was clean and modern. The *Buffalo*s were basically filled with the scraps from the other lines using the older equipment. I got an eighteen-inch long *Buffalo* that resulted from a slippage of the cutting machine.

Don Lelo had gathered a small group to go to Milparada to see the finished Comedor, including a photographer for *La Prensa*. Rafael drove. More significantly, Dr. Guillermo Bendano joined us. While he has been cordial with us students, he has expressed a negative attitude towards the poor. I took his presence as a positive sign that we are gaining support among the Rotarians. I'm afraid I stole center stage when we arrived. I was absolutely mobbed by the children, who were hoping that I had returned to stay. The meal went smoothly. Dr. Bendano was favorably impressed by how well it was organized and by how well the kids behaved.

Rafael dropped Lelo and me off in Cofradia. I had a long afternoon talk with Don Lelo, rehashing the summer and our future plans. After dinner, I entertained Nelly and her family with my guitar and singing.

Wednesday, August 25

Nelly took me to the San Pedro airport to check in by 9:00am for the SASHA DC-3 flight to Guatemala scheduled to leave at 10:00am. It actually left at 10:45am.

Shortly after I checked in, a gentleman brought a beautiful blonde over to meet me, telling her, "See there is another American on your flight. You can talk with him." This was my introduction to a real beauty queen. It was also the first time I had heard any English since the rest of the team left. She had spent a week in Honduras as part of her prize in winning the Miss Indiana Banana contest. She actually hailed from Dallas and was attending the University of Indiana. She was eager to talk, mostly to whine about conditions in Honduras. "Most of the people don't even speak English." "My hotel room didn't even have air conditioning, just a ceiling fan." And worst of all: "The electric sockets are a strange shape. I couldn't plug my hair dryer in." I tried to explain that, like much of Europe, Honduras used 220-volt electricity and it would have burned out the motor in her 110-volt hair dryer. It was hard enough to sit there and listen to her yammering, and impossible to feel any sympathy.

We landed at 11:45am. It only took five minutes to pick up my luggage and clear customs. A taxi took me to the Hotel Centro-America. I bought a bus ticket to Mexico City, with an overnight stop in Quezatango. The next bus was scheduled to leave at 3:00pm. I paid $1.00 for lunch and the privilege of keeping my luggage behind the front desk until the bus left. That left me with a little more than an hour to wander around the main market. Guatemala City struck me as amazingly large and modern. Downtown was choked by heavy traffic.

The bus was a modern Greyhound-type bus. It left promptly on time. The afternoon provided was a pleasant ride along the paved Pan American Highway through the mountains. I was purely a spectator looking out the window, so my observations are necessarily superficial. The peasants are almost one hundred percent Indian. They are better, and warmer dressed than in Honduras, except that most are wearing sandals, rather than shoes. I saw very little livestock and many unfenced fields. The fields are relatively large and well-plowed and at all stages of growth. Rice is growing on hillside terraces. The houses are adobe brick rather than *barareque* with more whitewash and paint, but fewer tile roofs.

We arrived in Quezatango at nightfall and checked into the Hotel Canada. The front desk clerk speaks English. The cost for a single room is $1.60 for a room plus a $.40 required tip. Dinner is $1.00 more. Shortly after I started dinner, an older, distinguished gentleman asked if he could join my table. After exchanging pleasantries, he told me that he is a professor of history at the local college. "Are you perhaps a student?"

"Yes. I am a studying mathematics."

"Where are you from?"

"Arizona, in the United States."

His eyes widened, obviously surprised. "I thought you must be from El Salvador or Nicaragua. You speak Spanish like a native, but your accent isn't Guatemalan."

I couldn't have received a higher compliment.

Thursday, August 26

I got up at 4:00am. The 4:30 bus left at 5:00am. This was the night bus, which had left Guatemala City at 12:30am, so the other passengers were asleep on board. It was COLD before sunup.

The corn crop had already been harvested in the area. Some stretches of the highway were unpaved, but being worked on. The landscape became more jungle-like near border. We made a brief Stop for breakfast at 8:00am, and reached the Mexican border at 8:30am. The bus from Mexico City had already arrived and its southbound passengers were waiting for us to get off.

The border inspection was slow and thorough. A couple of the passengers in front of me were turned back at the border. The person standing next to me said that they probably did not have cash equivalent to $100 U.S. with them. Nobody is allowed to enter Mexico without that much money. The Mexican government is very concerned about not having poor Central Americans come in and depress their economy or get free medical service. This news sent a wave of fear through my body. I have four twenty-dollar traveler's checks and enough mixed currency to equal a total of ninety-two dollars. (If I had known, I could have bought my ticket to the first stop in Mexico, then bought another ticket for the rest of the way.) I was wondering how long I would be stuck while I tried to get some money wired to me from home. Maybe I could sell my guitar for ten dollars. Fortunately for me, the law is not equally applied to all foreigners. When I showed my U.S. passport and pulled out the book of traveler's checks, I was passed through without a count. We finally got moving at 11:15am.

We were stopped for four more migration checks this afternoon; these were just a soldier checking our passports for a Mexican entry stamp. The land was swampy with lots of rivers, which we crossed on bridges. The landscape alternated between grassy pastures and jungle. Many men and boys we pass were shirtless. Our lunch stop didn't come until 4:00pm. There was no stated length for the stop. You just had to keep an eye on the drivers. Whenever he finished his meal, the trip resumed. The road was again paved, but as it went up into the mountains, it became narrower. In Mexico, it is the downhill vehicle that has right-of-way. The logic is that on many trucks the brakes are likely to fail, so the downhill driver probably couldn't stop if he wanted to. The lush vegetation thinned out as we rose. The top of the first plateau had terrain similar to Arizona desert – mostly agave and cacti. I have become friendly with a couple of Nicaraguan students who are going to attend the National University in Mexico City. As we drove through mountain villages, we engaged in some comparative girl-watching through windows.

We had a supper stop at 9:00pm and changed drivers. Another stop for a migration check, and now to sleep.

Friday, August 27

I woke up around 6:00am - dawn's early light comes later here than in Milparada. It was the best night's sleep I've ever had on a bus.

We were still in mountains. I witnessed the driver and his replacement trade places without stopping or even slowing down. At 6:30am we started dropping down into the central plateau. (It is only relatively flat.) The view of snowcapped Popocatepetl dominates the valley. We had breakfast in Puebla at 8:00am and pulled into Mexico City at 10:15. On first impression, Mexico City is huge, clean, rich and modern.

I took a taxi to Stu's address. (The Cornell student who had left an open invitation before I left New York.) It turned out that he's gone to Acapulco with friends, but I am still welcome to stay. I am thankful for the free bed, but don't want to impose any more than necessary. My plan was to buy a third class train ticket to Juarez on the border with Texas and then I can safely spend whatever is left for sightseeing. I took a bus to the Pemex Travel Service. They were almost useless, only wanting to sell first class travel. So I got directions to the train station and walked through the spacious and clean La Grimma market. Navigating the city streets was confusing; the street numbering is irregular and crossed two different "O" streets. I bought a moderate lunch for $1. Once I got to the train station and I had to stand in line for an hour to buy my ticket. The agent was surprised that a Norte Americano wanted third class and tried to get me to upgrade to at least second class. A store in the station advertised sight-seeing tours for $8.00. When I booked a tour for tomorrow I was told that the sign had an old price. That was irritating, but I figured that $12.00 for a full day tour was still a good deal. The guide will pick me up in the morning at the closest hotel to where I'm staying.

By the time I finished making the arrangements, it was raining hard. I couldn't get a taxi or bus to stop for more than an hour. All the ones that went by were full. I got back to Stu's for an awkward dinnertime conversation with his parents. I'm ready for a shower and early bed.

Saturday, August 28

I awoke at 5:00am, feeling sick to my stomach. My only choices were to go ahead with the sightseeing, or just lie in bed all day. This is my only chance to see Mexico City, so I decided to tough it out and hope that my stomach holds out.

Our tour started promptly at 9:00am. It was just a French couple, the guide and I. The guide spoke broken English, but he was a nice guy. I got better answers when I asked in Spanish. We covered a lot of ground starting with the huge Rivera murals at the National Palace and the National Cathedral. For all it history and fame, the massive Cathedral is ugly and sooty on the outside with all kinds of vendors harassing the tourists on the plaza. We could clearly see evidence that it is slowing sinking in the soft soil. The inside is beautiful. University City is all pretty. There were a bunch of skateboarders outside the stadium, which will host the next Olympics. The area next to the University is a lush residential section. All the houses are very modernistic (with prices of $64,000 and up). Our next stop was Chapultepec Castle and park. The park was being enjoyed by lots of locals, some just strolling, others having picnics. Our lunch was at a tourist trap near the pyramids with a century plant blooming in front. Lunch was good but cost $2.00 and any atmosphere was ruined by a lousy singer who "played" an empty box as a drum. At least my stomach had pretty well recovered.

The Aztec pyramids are impressive. They are far larger than the Mayan ruins in Copan. The Pyramid Del Sol (sun) has a base of over four hundred feet on a side and is almost two hundred feet tall. The climb to the top was tiring, it is steep and each step seemed to be eighteen inches tall. The guide waited at the bottom. Once at the top, I was rewarded with a spectacular view of the courtyard and slightly smaller Pyramid Del Luna (moon). The distant panorama included the twin dormant volcanoes Popocatepetl and Ixtacihuatl. The Shrine of the Lady of Guadalupe was most impressive point of the tour. The building is distinctly lopsided; perhaps it will become the next leaning tower of Pisa. The final hour was a required stop at classy and expensive shopping area. The tour company is paid to include it at the end of each tour. It has everything a tourist would want: a leather shop featuring fancy golf bags, a lacquer ware shop, glassblowers at work, onyx chess sets and oil-on-felt paintings. I had no money to buy any of it, but guide still needed to keep us there for the allotted time.

I got back to Stu's at 6:30am, thanked my hosts, picked up my bags and took a taxi to train station. I was practically broke once I paid the driver. I bought a stack of tortillas and a bottle of Coke, which left me with a total of four pesos (worth about eight cents apiece) and an American dime when I boarded the train. The train left on time at 7:50pm.

The third class seats are wood benches and the car has one toilet at each end. The car is full, but not overcrowded. Most of my fellow passengers are families with possessions bundled in blankets and baskets. They are visiting within the family groups, leaving me with a bench to myself. The train is well staffed with distinct roles indicated by their uniforms. The Conductors are strictly supervisors. *Auditors* take tickets. The *Garroteros* announce the stops as the train pulls in. The *Agentes* are vendors selling food and beverages. We also have two janitors who regularly sweep the cars and pick up trash.

Sunday, August 29

I slept poorly on the hard bench, especially since there were numerous jerky stops. It has been a long and tedious day on the train.

Early this morning, the scenery changed from forest to desert. The upper part of the desert was mostly prickly pear, then yucca and cholla cacti came to dominate. I saw a small irrigated farm area around Torreon at 5:30am. The houses there are mostly brown adobe brick with flat roofs. The peasants appear better fed and dressed than in Honduras.

Inside the train, most passengers passed the time having a big picnic. I still feel kind of sick – maybe it is at partially due to dehydration, but I don't want to take a chance on local water. My last four pesos went for three Cokes (bought through the window at different stops for a third of the price the on-board vendor charge) and a stack of three tortillas. The janitors swept out our car five different times during the day.

Monday, August 29

We had a long stop at Chihuahua at 12:30am. Armed officials came through the train checking papers. My foreign passport in the third class car evoked suspicions; I was grilled about where I was coming from and where I was going. We arrived in Juarez at 5:30am and I walked the half-mile to the El Paso border station.

Not surprisingly, I was pulled aside for a thorough inspection by the custom officials. The questioning started with "How far down are you coming from?" I filled in the custom form with a complete list of everything I had acquired outside the United States and what I had paid for them: One quart of guaro ($2.50), one machete ($5), one carved wood Mayan statue $1.50, one seed-pod necklace ($.50), one homemade cake of soap (free gift), one small basket (free gift). My super-long cigarette hadn't survived the trip. By the time they finished with me, it was almost 8:00am. I used my last dime in the pay phone to call my grandmother. She arrived in fifteen minutes in the brand new Cadillac that she had gotten yesterday. I could see the open-mouthed stares of two custom agents as we pulled away. I wondered what they were thinking.

I was groggy as we ate a big breakfast: cantaloupe, waffles, eggs and sausage, with orange juice and coffee. Conversing in English, especially without using cuss words, took a little getting used to. My grandmother was wonderfully accepting. I took a shower then slept all day. When I woke up for dinner, all my clothes were clean and dry.

I have so many things to tell her and the rest of the family, and I have so much to sort through in my mind before I can explain them to anyone.

October 1965

I got a neatly hand printed note from Honduras today:

Milparada 20 of September/65

The Youth Ricardo Galbraith

New York

Unforgettable Richard

   I am filled with pride by having received your friendly note today, but it also makes me proud to know that, although you are far away, you treat me like a brother. That relationship is unprecedented for me in my entire life, knowing you.

   My brother, since you left this humble village we have felt the lack of your presence and not only I. I can say for everyone that this place has stayed like a desert, saying nothing else. Aah, we so miss the people from Cornell! But though it is impossible to have you all by our side and you had to leave, we still have hopes that you all return next year because we have asked the being supreme to grant to us a return visit from you. Brother, I have enjoyed the account of your trip, and we give thanks to God for you not having troubles on your trip to the U.S. territory.

   Brother, all of those in our house are well, working as always, going to our field with memories of you. My Good parents greet you with affection and say that for them it was a big pleasure to have had you stay in our house. Also, greetings from Tina, Delia, Jorge, Carlos and Bartito, who says he will never forget you.

   Brother, with respect to the school's dining center, I give you the good news that it has been functioning well. From the 16th to this date, it is feeding between 60 and 75 children from all around the village. Don Lelo has come here more than eight days to be sure that that the dining room is working well. It is always a memory of all of you. All of your friends who met you send their greeting, and I send a strong hug with which says ever since we said farewell I have hoping to hear from you, and through you I send greetings to all the members of the team of Cornell.

Good-bye, little brother

Marcos Hernandez

We have also gotten word through Nelly and Don Lelo that an official from CARE inspected the *comedor* and its operation. It passed with flying colors and now the service has been expanded to include preschoolers as well as current students. That explains the increase in the lunch count to seventy-five. This news has me fired up to support next year's project.

I have just finished compiling our team's official report for the Cornell United Religious Works board of directors. I've included the summary here:

The Value to Milparada

Milparada received some concrete benefits: the *comedor*, school desks and supplies, medical service, etc. Worthy achievements? Yes, but not enough to justify the effort. The key accomplishment of the summer was the formation of the *"Comite Milparada Hacia el Progreso."* For the first time, townspeople were joined together to help themselves. We had planned for the committee to run the *comedor*, but the town wouldn't stop there. They had some models for civic improvements: the *comedor*, the new school, the garden, the team's way of living, and the progressive village of Pinalejo. They had a few resources: they had been introduced to CARE and the Alliance for Progress, and they had the materials we would leave them. And, they had dreams, which now they think they can make come true. Time will tell to what extent they succeed, but in any event, Cornell has left behind a new way of tackling problems, and a new hope . . . a higher horizon.

Looking back over the summer, we see the child feeding center standing in Milparada as a symbol of what we, as a group, stood for – an attempt to begin toward a better way of life, a more sound life, and perhaps a longer life. (The current average life span in Honduras is forty years.) And to carry the symbol farther, we could state that the juxtaposition of the *comedor* and the school indicates the inter-relatedness of progress and education.

Yet, it is quite unfair to say that there are only problems in an existence of the sort found in Milparada. The people have found happiness in many ways. Children still play; people still love. Nor can we close our minds to the positive aspects in the area of health. While most certainly not done for health reasons, the corn used to make tortillas is soaked in lime water, thus supplying calcium in the diet. Also, at present, the progressive schoolteachers have the kids planting a garden behind the school. Planting of gardens is little done in the area – perhaps the people haven't learned how easily good nutrition could be had. If they lack seeds, CARE or AFP will provide them. There was only one woman who asked us for seeds to plant. Another woman explained that while they liked vegetables when they had them, it was too much work to plant them – a rather *"que sera, sera"* attitude.

San Pedro and the Rotary Club

A vital part of the program was the time spent in San Pedro Sula. From a material standpoint, our work would have been impossible without the resources available in San Pedro. Beyond this, the contact with the businessmen and professionals, the upper-class of Honduras, gave the team a much more balanced view of the country than they could get in Milparada alone.

One of the original aims of the project was to get the rich and educated Hondurans involved in helping the poor of their own country. To a certain extent, this has worked. The San Pedro Rotary Club has been the project's host in Honduras for five years. This year, they spent over $600 to help our work. However, less than half the members were really involved in the project. In an effort to improve on this, we tried to get Rotarians to come out and see what was being done. We had a qualified success. Only seven of the forty odd Rotarians came (two of whom either had no previous contact with the project or were opposed to it), but this was still seven more than had visited Cornell teams the previous year. In addition, local enthusiasm reached a point where several people, Rotarians and others, decided that they ought to continue the project, at least nominally, throughout the year. Therefore, we helped organize the *"Comite Honduras y Cornell"*, a ten member coordinating committee to make advance arrangements for Cornell teams and to continue to assist the towns after the team leaves.

The Value to the Participant

The Cornell-Central America Project is educational beyond any measure of grades and credit hours. In a sense, it comes much closer to the ideal Liberal Arts education than any college in the U.S. The participant is freed from the artificial breakdown of the world into Government, History, Anthropology, Sociology, Agriculture, etc.; all of these are bound together in the curriculum of a new environment, with a different economy, a different set of values, and a different way of thinking than any of the students have encountered before. He may have read of them, but it is much more valuable to grapple with problems head-on than to intellectualize about them in protected seclusion. The student is forced to realize the extent to which he has been culture-bound. He learns how many "necessities" he can live without, and he learns how much he can do on his own. He gains a new perspective, added self-confidence, and increased intellectual independence. From a more purely academic standpoint, he attends a Spanish class about ten hours every day, and through the combination of preparatory readings, seminars, discussions, and first-hand experience, he learns a great deal about the history, government and economy of Honduras, and about the culture of the *campesino*. Also, the student is well paid, not with money, because the people in the villages don't have much, but with love and appreciation.

The eight members of the team invested about $400 each, a semester of preparation, and an entire summer vacation to receive eight weeks of hard work, poor living conditions and numerous frustrations. Yet, if we had it to do over again, every one of us would choose to go down again. Why? It is partly because of the friends we made, partly because we feel that we have done something worthwhile, and partly because we know the experience has improved us.

In evaluating the project, we should look at two components: what we gave, and what we got. Our work this summer didn't change the world, or even Honduras. It wasn't supposed to. But it did change each one of us, and it did start the people of Milparada on a road to betterment which, hopefully, they will continue to travel.

Our team unanimously agreed on a proposal for next year:

A plan for the 1966 Project in the North Coast Region

The 1965 Milparada team recommends that a 12 man team be sent to the North Coast region of Honduras to work in the villages of Milparada and Chiquila during the summer of 1966.

Four students, a boy with training in agriculture and one with experience in accounting, a registered nurse with training in public health, and a student of either the School of Nutrition or Home Economics, will live in Milparada to expand on the work done by previous teams. The program is designed to make the village less dependent on Cornell for future improvements. The following are suggested projects:

1.   Organize an agricultural co-op to improve farming techniques and to buy local corn for storage until prices go up. Help is available from Fernando Montez and the Christian Democrats, from CUNA for organization problems, from STICA for technical aid, and perhaps from U.S. Ambassador Jova for initial capital.'

2.   Set up a *"Club de Amas de Casa"* (homemakers club) through which instruction in health, nutrition, child care, cooking (the *comedor* can serve as a model kitchen), etc. This group could also start a campaign for family vegetable gardens (seeds available from SCIDE).

3.   Assist the *"Comite Milparada Hacia el Progreso"* in any projects they desire (e.g. Expanding the water system), and introduce its officers to the resources (staff of CARE, etc.) available in San Pedro.

4.   Administer necessary medical treatment.

5.   Work with the Alliance Health Team to initiate an extensive latrine building program.

A group of eight students, similar to the 1965 Milparada Team, will live in Chiquila, a small town west of Milparada, to oversee the construction of a new school and to convert the old one into a CARE *comedor*. Secondary projects, like a literacy program and recreation classes will be operated on the basis of perceived need and available time.

Our discussions with Hayword have already had an influence on the direction of the program. The Recruiting materials are primarily describing the experience as "a summer of hard work to trigger community development," with the goodwill and increased international understanding being side effects.

April 1966

Our whole team got together for Juan's wedding in Rochester. We assumed that it would be a grand feast and party. Our high expectations were crushed when we got to the reception. The bride's parents put on a tasteful spread featuring finger sandwiches and fruit punch – not a drop of alcohol in the place. Although we had a good time reminiscing, it was clear that we were drifting apart as we pursued our diverse career plans. Also, like the rest of the college students, the Vietnam war and the draft has become the center of our immediate social concerns. I am the only one of us who is still actively involved in the program.

Our team's proposal for a specialized follow up team in Milparada had to be scrapped. From talking with Peace Corps officials about their experiences in setting up cooperatives, we came to realize that we had badly underestimated the time required to get the proper incorporation and accounting procedures in place, especially in a town where no one had ever kept even a simple bookkeeping ledger. Nevertheless, our support from our Honduran hosts has grown and our recruiting was successful. Our proposal for Chiquila is firmly in place. Thanks to Don Lelo and Nelly, the townspeople are already starting to make bricks for the new school. The project is also expanding into the urban slums of Tegucigalpa with an additional team.

The one big dark cloud has been finances. Several likely foundations have chosen not to grant our applications, mainly because of commitments they have made to Civil Rights projects in the United States. Last month, the local paper reported our imminent demise.

The Cornell Daily Sun

Friday, March 25, 1966

Lack of Funds May End Univ. Latin America Project

By SUSAN A. NEWMARK

Jack Lewis, director of Cornell United Religious Works announced last night that unless definite financial support is in sight for the Cornell - in - Central America Project by the end of the first week in April, the project will have to be abandoned.

Lewis is hopeful that positive word will be received from a foundation by then, though.

The previous deadline of this weekend for a decision on the Central America Project was extended by Lewis, in conjunction with Thomas H. Lodahl, outgoing chairman of the CURW board, and Mark Barlow, vice president for student affairs.

The Brazil project has received pledges for a substantial amount of its budget already, it was announced last night at the CURW annual board meeting. The East Harlem project will definitely be carried out this summer, even though definite financial support has not yet been obtained.

In other business . . .

Part of the other business was the election of the Board of Directors. I am now on that board. This week we got the great news that we have received a renewable grant from some foundation that I had never heard of. To meet their criteria, the official primary goal of the teams is back to "improving international relationships." At this point, I don't care what they call it. We are back in business.

September 1966

This summer's Chiquila team was a huge success. The three-room school building that the teacher and I drafted on paper is now a reality. The men of the village had the bricks ready before the team arrived and worked along with the team throughout the construction period.

I was even more gratified to hear that they had paid a visit to Milparada, where we were fondly remembered. More importantly, the *comedor* is still operating.

We have clearly developed a niche where a group of college student volunteers can make a significant and lasting contribution to community development.

February 1967

Disaster has struck. The New York Times broke a story identifying a bunch of organizations as CIA fronts. Listed along with some export companies and charter aircraft outfits as the name of the foundation that provided our major funding for the last two years. My first reaction was disbelief. Why would the CIA be involved with what we were doing? Our totally non-political work with the poor can't have any relevance to CIA operations. We checked with all of the team members. None of them had been interviewed by any government officials or strangers on their return. The CIA hasn't reaped any intelligence from their investment in us. Nevertheless, the Cornell-in-Central America Project is now tainted by our supposed association with the CIA. I'm worried about the effect on my own reputation.

Worse yet, the press in Latin America picked up the story with just enough details to brand our student volunteers as spies or CIA operatives. Even if we could find another source of funds, the members of the Rotary Club and the other locals whose support is vital to our success cannot afford to be associated with the project.

The Cornell-in-Central America project is dead. It was killed by the stupidity of one of our government's bureaucracies.

Aftermath in Harlem

At Cornell, we returned from Christmas vacation for two weeks of classes and final exams, followed by a five day break so the professors could complete their paperwork and grading before the second semester started. This schedule was fine for students with the money and inclination to go skiing, but since the dorms were closed for the break, it created a problem for those of us who were a long way from home and on a tight budget.

Once again, Cornell United Religious Works provided a way for me to fill the schedule hole with an exciting opportunity. The center piece of the East Harlem Project was a camp program that brought underprivileged kids from East Harlem to campus for two weeks of tutoring and fun activities led by student mentors during the summer, then a follow-up program for the college participants to spend the winter break in Harlem getting a first-hand look at the "War on Poverty" while re-connecting with the campers. Technically, I wasn't eligible for the trip, but I talked my way in as a substitute for one the mentors who dropped out.

I was introduced to Wilfredo at the Harlem Y. He was a thin fourteen year-old with a complexion the color of semi-sweet chocolate, shiny black hair, and a big smile. I awkwardly shook his hand and apologized for his mentor's absence. He quickly took over the conversation. He was enthusiastic about the week he had spent at Cornell; though he had much more to say about all the trees and open space than about whatever the program had been. His high school classes were mostly boring, but he wanted to finish school so he could get a good job. He appeared to be a strikingly normal kid; nothing marked him as "underprivileged".

We spent the next four days touring different agencies and anti-poverty programs, hearing about the problems they faced and the good things they were doing, or at least attempting. Most of the stories were anecdotal. I heard very little hard evidence of improvements. The urban renewal projects were depressingly sterile. The occupants seemed to lock themselves in with their televisions. Still they had long waiting lists of people seeking rat-free apartments with working plumbing and elevators. I decided that I would rather live in a broken down tenement building with a vest pocket park on the corner where I could hang out with my neighbors. The tours culminated with attendance at a Sunday morning service in Adam Clayton Powell's church. I had been looking forward to hearing him speak on Civil Rights. His actual preaching mostly consisted on name dropping, reminding the congregation of how well he was connected to the powers that be in Washington and in city government. Maybe he had improved things in the past, but I only witnessed his self-aggrandizement. Over the whole week we had heard optimistic rhetoric supported only by a small number of well-meaning people attempting to change a grim reality. I don't think anyone knows how to actually create a Great Society.

The former campers rejoined us on the last afternoon for a Circle Line boat tour. It was Wilfredo's first time on a boat of any sort. I found myself in the strange position of being a tourist who was pointing out the sights to a native. The planned sights were overshadowed by spotting a bloated dead body floating face down in the East River. I kept my eye on it in our wake until a Coast Guard boat hooked it on a long pole. By then, it was too far away to see any details. Wilfredo paid much less attention to it than I did. He was more interested in talking to me than in the sights. As we approached the dock, he asked if I would write him. I gave him my address and told him that I would answer any letter he sent me.

Surprisingly, he did write. As Spring Break approached, I had another hole to fill. A classmate invited me to stay with his family in Washington D.C. starting on Monday. That left me a weekend to kill off campus. I decided to stop over in New York City, staying at the Harlem Y, since it was by far the cheapest room I could find in town. I wrote to Wilfredo and invited him out Sunday to lunch and the matinee at Radio City Music Hall. In return, he invited me to have dinner with his family. He showed up promptly at 9:00am. The day was still cold enough that my ski jacket was a necessary part of my attire. We walked the length of Central Park, bought hot dogs from a stand for lunch. We arrived at Radio City only to discover that it was closed. (It was the week after Easter.) I was totally taken aback by this affront and had no idea of what to do to entertain Wilfredo for the afternoon. We walked on over by Times Square, where he spotted a couple of run-down theaters showing adventure films. The price was right, so I agreed to the one he chose. I had second thoughts as soon as we entered. All of the other customers were men, many of them looking like they were using the ticket price as a cheap way to keep warm after a night on the streets. The place also smelled of stale booze. Wilfredo seemed oblivious to these distractions, so we sat where no one else was near us and "enjoyed" the B-movie. As soon as the movie ended, we moved on to the subway, which now seemed like a clean, safe location, and went back up to Spanish Harlem.

Wilfredo lived on 128th Street, east of Park Avenue. The street is a solid row of five and six story tenement houses from the last century. We passed a semi-conscious drunk leaning against the doorway to enter the grungy, stale smelling entry way. Then it was up four flights of stairs to an unlit hallway and the door to his apartment. After we knocked and Wilfredo identified himself, I heard a series of four different locks turned before the door opened. My first impression of the apartment was that I had stepped into a Dickens novel. The kitchen was at one end of the main room and included a bathtub covered by a slab-door to make it the dining room table. The toilet was in a small closet next to the kitchen. The other end of the room was furnished with a pair of broken down sofas, an end table and a small black-and-white television. The two windows looked down on a trash filled courtyard. Doors at the end of the room led to two small bedrooms.

The initial introductions were awkward; I felt like an intruder from another country. Wilfredo's mother and grandmother were working in the kitchen. His grandfather came over from his chair to shake my hand; his aunt and sister (about 12 years old) did likewise. Three smaller boys, probably nephews watched me cautiously from the sofa. Nine people lived in the two bedroom apartment; obviously there weren't enough beds to go around. Wilfredo slept on the sofa, with zero privacy and no place to do homework without constant distractions from the younger kids.

The grandparents spoke only Spanish. The atmosphere relaxed considerably when I switched to Spanish to converse with them. The adults and Wilfredo gathered around the "table" for dinner. The kids got their plates and sat on the sofa or floor in front of the TV to eat. Dinner was basically a plate of seasoned rice, beans and stewed tomatoes. Wilfredo's mother was apologetically concerned that it was inadequate. I took one bite and reassured her that it was good, reminding of the dinners we cooked when I was in Honduras. That comment opened the way for a couple of hours of cheerful conversation.

Grandmother talked extensively about her life in Puerto Rico, how green everything was and how pleasant the village life was. But there are no jobs there now. The family had to move or go hungry. In New York, there were jobs for everyone. Her husband works in a restaurant and both daughters have jobs sewing in a clothing factory, while she stays home and watches the little ones. The jobs are hard work and they are tired all the time, but they can feed everybody. She doesn't think they will ever get better jobs, but if their children can finish school, they will have an opportunity to do better. Back in Puerto Rico, there are no opportunities for the young. I was happy to encourage their hopes for Wilfredo's future.

It was 9:00pm before I knew it; time for the little ones to get ready for bed and for me to pick up my bags from the Y and head on to the bus station. Sleeping on the bus to Washington would save me the cost of a room for the night. Wilfredo's mother suggested that he go with me to the subway station to see that I got there safely. The idea of a college male needing an escort from a child to walk four blocks struck me as silly. I politely declined the offer and said my good-byes.

It was a cool, quiet evening as I strolled down the dark, empty street. I was almost to Park Avenue when a knot of teenage black boys came around the corner. Some gym or arcade must have just closed. I stepped aside to let them pass. One of them stepped in front of me. His voice was angry, "Hey nigger, what are you doing here?"

I was shocked at being called nigger, but tried to sound nonchalant. "I just finished having dinner at a friend's house and now I'm headed home."

"This is our turf, nigger. You don't belong here."

"I'm leaving – just passing through."

By now, I was surrounded. All eight to twelve of them were crowded around me with random calling out of "Nigger." I could not see any of their faces clearly. I was afraid, more scared than I can ever remember being. The leader announced, "We are going to rob you, nigger. We are going to take all your money."

"If I had any money, I wouldn't be walking in this part of town. I would have taken a cab." That wasn't exactly true; I had a little over twenty dollars in my wallet, and was wondering if I could have gotten a cab to pick me up in this neighborhood. Still, it seemed to work. The yells of "Nigger" stopped. The leader looked me in the eye and took a step back. Then, CRACK – somebody from behind broke a bottle over my head and I collapsed on the sidewalk. Someone kicked me hard. I curled up into as much of a ball as I could so my padded ski jacket offered some protection from the blows. As the kicks and yells of "Nigger" continued, I wondered if I would survive or if the discovery of my body would make the newspapers. I was fading into semi-consciousness when I heard, "Hey you kids, get away from here."

Then it got quiet. Two large black men holding tire irons sent the teens fleeing. They gently lifted me to a standing position and asked if I was alright. I wasn't sure. They helped me to the parking garage where they worked, got the glass out of my head, washed the wound and gave me a rag to hold on my head to stop the bleeding. My back, especially around the kidneys ached. My head throbbed and there was a constant buzzing in my ears. I was woozy and uncertain how long I would remain conscious. Through the fog, I could hear a kindly baritone voice muttering, "Those darned kids. I don't know why they would do something like this…"

After a while, a pair of cops arrived and the situation changed from painful to surreal. After recounting the incident to the officers, they discussed among themselves their next action. They could either take me four blocks to the Bellevue Emergency room, or they could drive me to the precinct house a mile away and have an ambulance pick me up there. The senior officer's stated logic was, "Since it is a head injury, it might be serious. So we better have an ambulance respond." I would have expected the "it might be serious" diagnosis to have been a reason to get me to immediate medical care, rather than justification for a detour to the police office.

Once I got in the back of the police car, I got a stern lecture about the stupidity of ever coming into that part of town or of walking anywhere in New York after dark. "What were you doing around here anyways?"

"I was having dinner with a friend in his apartment."

"Another bleeding-heart social worker?"

"No. I'm a college student."

"We're going to drive around the neighborhood and look for the kids who attacked you. So look out the window and point any of them out." So much for the concern that my head injury might be serious...

"I told you I couldn't recognize any of them. It was dark and I didn't get a good look at anyone before I got hit."

"That's OK. Just point out anyone who looks like the boys that mugged you. It doesn't matter if he was the ones who attacked this time. All of them are guilty of something."

"I couldn't do that. There's no way I could say I recognized the attackers."

"Another bleeding-heart liberal."

We drove the rest of the way to the precinct house in silence. Once there, I was given a seat on a hard wood bench in the entry room and left to wait for forty-minutes, still holding the bloody rag against my head. I was feeling more animosity towards the cops than for the teens that attacked me. Once the ambulance responded, it was a short ride to the hospital where I was wheeled directly into an examining room. In fairly short order, I got a pain pill, twelve stitches in my scalp and had my head X-rayed. The admissions desk then filled out a form with my name, address and insurance information and told me it would take about thirty minutes before they had a report on my X-rays. I checked back more than an hour later, asking what my X-ray showed.

"Oh are you still here?" was the surprise response. The nurse made a phone call and informed me that the X-rays had already been sent to storage. She explained that most of the victims of knife or gunshot wounds gave false names and disappeared. They just took X-rays and filled in the forms to meet the health department's certification rules. After another half-hour, I had the X-ray with a notation that there was no skull damage and instructions to have the stitches removed in a week to ten days. I was able to retrieve my bag from the YMCA and catch a bus from Penn Station that got me to Washington and my roommate's house in time for breakfast.

Needless to say, his mother was shocked by my initial appearance. After I got cleaned up, I had a relaxing and enjoyable week with their family.

I did exchange one more round of letters with Wilfredo that spring, making no mention of the mugging. The only long term effect of that night was that I could no longer enjoy walking in a big city at night. For the next ten years, I would grow tense and nervous whenever I approached a dark alleyway or corner.

Three years later, I drove down to New York City with my girl friend for a big date, a Broadway matinee followed by dinner. We had just left the show and started walking toward the parking garage when I heard a voice call out my name:

"Hey Dick! Is your name Dick?"

I turned to see a large, menacing-looking teen in a black leather jacket approaching us.

"Do you remember me? Freddie ... Wilfredo. You took me to a movie."

"Oh – yes. You've really grown a lot."

"I graduated and I am starting college at City College."

"That's great..." I'm stunned and wondering what to say next.

"I've got to get going to my job in a restaurant. I just wanted to say thank you."

Photographs

Milparada's laundry area where the road from Quimistan crosses the river.

The Cornell Team: Susan, Doug, Dick, Juan, Mary and Melissa, plus a neighbor. (Trinchi is taking the picture.)

The plaza in Milparada. The team lived in the two houses in the foreground on the left.

Afternoon rain, from the "porch" of our house.

Eduardo Dubon's corn field. The best bottom land in town.

Marcos Hernandez's Milpa (slash and burn farming).

School Assembly singing the Honduran National Anthem. The first grade classroom, crowded with the students from both Milparada and Quimistan.

I am in the front with *Profesora* Maria Luisa and *Profesor* Jacobo.

A finished CARE desk. David and Oscar Machado are helping me carry it to the school.

The school children preparing their vegetable garden.

Doug pouring cement into the first column for the *comedor*.

Raising the *comedor* roof trusses. I am on top on the left.

The finished *comedor* and school building.

The boa constrictor that one of the young farmers killed in his field.

Don Pedro Hernandez at the Castillo de San Fernando in Omoa.

Roberto Escalon standing in the doorway of his family's *jacale* home.

The Hernandez family in front of their *barareque* home. From left to right: Delia, Claudio, Tina, Jesus, next door neighbor, Jorge Nineco, Margareta Nineco de Hernandez, Carlos, Bartito Nineco, Julian, and Marcos.

Acknowledgements

This narrative is a recent reconstruction. My detailed notes from 1965 have sat in a notebook on my shelf for decades. While my notes were comprehensive, they contained few complete sentences and liberal use of my personal short hand. They were also only partially organized. All of the team members contributed to a team log and to our final report. I have made liberal use of those documents in preparing this work. Therefore, I must share the credit for the information (as well as for our successes) to the amazingly talented and dedicated people who shared this experience: Juan Castro, Katrina Clark, Melissa Douglas, Douglas Dugan, Mary Elizabeth Englerth, Susan Porter and Edward Seeger.

A number of details are dated. Honduras has added a second hydro-electric dam and paved the highway between San Pedro Sula and Tegucigalpa. Unfortunately, most of the improvements have bypassed the subsistence farmers in the remote villages. Their daily lives have changed little in more than a century.

A word about prices: Minimum wage jobs in the United States were paying about $1.65 at the time. Based on that, I would multiply all of the references to costs by four, to get a realistic comparison to today's dollar. Inflation has hit Honduras harder than the United States. In 1965 the exchange rate was two Lempiras for a dollar. In 2008 the rate is nineteen Lempiras for a dollar.